Intimate
with the
Infinite

*To JUNE
Thank you for
your consistent
support
[signature] Kay
June 3/22/24*

Michael D. Johnson M.D.

ISBN 978-1-68570-456-8 (paperback)
ISBN 978-1-68570-457-5 (digital)

Christian Faith Publishing
832 Park Avenue
Meadville, PA 16335
www.christianfaithpublishing.com

Printed in the United States of America

To the five most important people in my life. They all happen to be women: first, my grandmother, affectionately known as Nannie, who taught me how to love the word of God and memorize scriptures; my mother, Helen, who taught me the love of reading and creating and the importance of poetry; my aunt Roberta, who taught me to never settle for less than my best; my mother-in-law, Susie Mae, who has lived a godly life, making it possible for me to have a godly wife; and of course, my godly wife, Sandra Kay, who was used by God to protect me and help me mature in my faith. Together these five women taught me to be sensitive and desire to be a man who honors God, seeking integrity in professional and personal life. Intimacy with the Infinite is what I have seen in the lives of these five women. Them modeling Christ before me is the true inspiration for me to model Him before others.

Foreword

These days, many professing Christians think only of their personal relationship with one another and consequently wander loosely without regard for their relationship with Christ. This book from beginning to its end addresses closeness to our Savior and a walk with Him that reaches levels of love beyond belief.

God has designed that we be joined not only to each other but to Him as well. The New Testament metaphors that depict Christ are richly instructive in carrying the weight of this great challenge. A challenge to be, "intimate with the infinite."

God calls us to be—intimate with Him and joins in the joy of love by loving us unconditionally.

What is intimacy with God?

1. A holy and royal priesthood offering spiritual sacrifices to God
2. A chosen race belonging to God
3. A spiritual nation whose king is the eternal God
4. A temple indwelt by the spirit of God
5. A set of branches connected to Jesus as the vine
6. A body of which the Lord Jesus is Head

All these metaphors feature the common characteristics of "intimacy with God"

Believers compose of the priesthood, one nation, one race, one temple, one plant, one flock, one family, and one body. We have all been made one spiritually, and we belong together in intimacy with God.

This helpful book lays out the crucial pattern for conduct in the fellowship that leads to the fulfillment of love. Love God with a blood-sealed love, born out of His blood He gave for us on the cross. Love Him with all your heart.

—Pastor James A. Lovett II
Tasker Street Missionary Baptist Church

Come Die with Me

My sweet savior bid
Your life is no good
'Till in Me it's hid
Die to your pleasures

Die to your pain
To your earthly treasures
The things you count gain
Die to your pride

Die to your rights
In Me fully abide
On Me set your sights
For too long you contest

For too long you strive
Give in to this death
Submit and come alive
Lose yourself in My will

Lose yourself to My way
If you are dead, just be still
I will indwell you that day
Come die, My sweet child

Take your last selfish breath
Let My spirit inside
Let My life give you rest

> For to me to live is Christ, and to die is gain.
> (Phil 1:21)
> For ye are dead, and your life is hid with
> Christ in God. (Col 3:3)

Appealing or Appalling

I find it revealing
As I hear my God calling
What I find appealing
My God finds appalling

So comfortable with sin
When I should be groaning
I strike a big grin
While my God is moaning

The world says it's right
Feed the flesh with all pleasures
So to end this flesh fight
Know that I'm His true treasure

He has placed His own sealing
He is continually drawing
God makes me appealing
So I could avoid the appalling

> Love not the world, neither the things that are in the world. If any man love the world, the love of the Father is not in him.
>
> For all that is in the world, the lust of the flesh, and the lust of the eyes, and the pride of life, is not of the Father, but is of the world. (1 Jn 2:15–16 King James Version [KJV])

I Want It All

I want it all, not what you can spare
Not the remnants you don't want
I am not asking you to share
I want it all—don't tease and don't taunt

I am jealous, and I will not take some
You attempt to placate, appease
I find it offensive, not worthy of notice
Bend your heart and not your knees

Not the prayer position or posture
Not the appearance that others might see
I consider half measures, you impostor
I want it all; it all belongs to Me

You keep some aside for your just in case
You squander; you hoard and collect
Your giving is not sacrifice; it's a disgrace
Your generous offering I do reject

I gave you all without measure or merit
I poured My life's blood; I suffered and died
I withheld nothing so you could have heaven
You withhold and give less; you have lied

I want it all, and the promise I give
Is you will have even more; this is true
Give Me all; that is how My child must live
All that I am I give freely to you

> *He* who *did not spare his* own *Son*, but gave
> him up for us all—how will *he not* also, along

with him, graciously give us all things? (Rom 8:32, emphasis added)

Again, the kingdom of heaven is like a merchant seeking beautiful pearls, who, when he had found one pearl of great price, went and sold all that he had and bought it. (Mt 13:45–46)

The Next Breath

Am I worthy of the next breath?
Will I just abuse this air?
Will I squander the grace You gave me,
Or will I generously share?

Will I seek the purpose You have?
Will I lift up those who've fallen,
Or will I continue self-pleasure?
Will I ignore Your voice that's calling?

You bid my heartbeat once more
You allowed me to breathe again
Will I use this very next moment
So others You win?

Am I worthy of the next breath,
Or will I just this air abuse?
Holy Spirit, give me strength
Within my lungs infuse

The strength to speak out loud
And with my final breath declare
That in Jesus only is life
Father, thank You for that air

> And the LORD God formed man of the dust
> of the ground, and breathed into his nostrils the
> breath of life; and man became a living soul. (Gn
> 2:7 KJV)

Makes Sense

Makes more sense to be smiling and rich
Than it does to be crying and poor
And that is why I made the switch
To serve Jesus, I get so much more

It is preached in all congregations
At least the services I do attend
Jesus has such high recommendations
On social media, He is the new trend

You will live in great comfort and ease
You will never suffer loss or distress
Have money to do all that you please
Jesus promised believers no stress

So with this thinking I decided *Why not?*
Gave my heart, with getting rich in mind
But it seemed that Jesus somehow forgot
To reveal the fine print I signed

Oh yes, this true abundance is clear
Overflowing, much more than expected
But the things He was giving abundantly
Were the very things I had rejected

Abundance of humility, quiet servanthood
Gracious giving without recognition
Not trying to win arguments or be understood
Not trying to be first in position

I call this a bait and switch scheme at best
Jesus said to win, pursue loss
I found the switch was my place of true rest
I embraced Him as Lord at His cross

> And he said to them all, If any man will
> come after me, let him deny himself, and take
> up his cross daily, and follow me. For whosoever
> will save his life shall lose it: but whosoever will
> lose his life for my sake, the same shall save it.
> (Lk 9:23–24)

The Enemy Is Dead

The headlines of the newspapers read
Sleep better now—our enemy's dead
Indeed, oh my, we finally got him
Blew himself up before we shot him
Let's get back to entertainment instead

The man on the breaking news said
Active shooter—keep low and cover your head
The police are now in hot pursuit
However, he is still able to shoot
I groaned and got back in bed

Be careful where you step or tread
In mosque where your prayer rug is spread
In church or synagogue when praying
Make "Keep us safe" the words you're saying
Give us comfort as our daily bread

Delightful Deprivation

Lord, whenever I face temptation
Give me the joy of delightful deprivation
Soothing, soft, seductive voices
Make it hard to make good choices
Give me escape from evil situations

Lord, I constantly feel such greed
Wanting more than I could ever need
Filling every closet, every shelf
Concerned with nothing more than self
Insatiable worldly appetites I constantly feed

Lord, how long must I abide
By a self-centered nature of my pride
Thinking others are beneath me
Dear Jesus, please bequeath me
Your humbling presence by my side

Lord, crush my appetite for fame
Increase my hunger for Your name
Give me the victory of Your presence
The holiness that is Your essence
And victory in You I will proclaim

> Psalm 91
>
> You will not fear the terror of night, nor
> the arrow that flies by day, nor the pestilence
> that stalks in the darkness, nor the plague that
> destroys at midday.

A thousand may fall at your side, ten thousand at your right hand, but it will not come near you.

Matthew 24:21-22 For then there will be great distress, unequaled from the beginning of the world until now—and never to be equaled again.

22 "If those days had not been cut short, no one would survive, but for the sake of the elect those days will be shortened.

Remove far from me vanity and lies: give me neither poverty nor riches; feed me with food convenient for me. (Prv 30:8)

There hath no temptation taken you but such as is common to man: but God is faithful, who will not suffer you to be tempted above that ye are able; but will with the temptation also make a way to escape, that ye may be able to bear it. (1 Cor 10:13)

Three Visits, One Visitor

My Comforter came by last evening
He pulled me close to His side
I felt warm within His embrace
From the angry world I now could hide

He hugged and softly caressed me
His smile and His touch felt so sweet
He massaged my emotion-worn body
From my head to the soles of my feet

My Lover stayed the whole night
He covered me with personal care
His whispering helped me sleep soundly
It felt good that my Savior was there

His kind and gentle demeanor
Pulled and tugged at my heart
I knew He would meet all my needs
He'd never, not ever, depart
My Father awakened me this morning

He asked me how was my rest
He said, "Today has challenges"
And He would be with me in each test

Three visitors, with one single agenda
One Godhead, one Trinity
One vision, purpose, will
To save and sanctify me

O visit me with Thy salvation. (Ps 106:4)

Sharing with My Lover

What a joy to share with my Lover
His tender caress and gentle care
To rest under His perfect cover
To know I can always stay there

It is His love that draws me close
It is His grace that pulls at my heart
It's in His love that I can boast
He promised He'd never leave me apart
It feels so good to know He's truly all mine

To depend on His kind and gentle touch
To feel His thoughts invade and possess my mind
There is nothing that thrills me quite so much

What a lover He is!

    I am my beloved's, And my beloved is
mine. (Song of Solomon 6:3)

A Kind Word

Did I say a little kind word
As I left you home today?
Did I stop and smile and hug you?
Or did I simply walk away?

Did I ring to say "I love you"?
Did I hold you up in prayer?
Or did I just assume that
Tonight you would be there?

Oh, the day is so uncertain
Each event and hour flies
And before long it is dark
And too late we realize

That we may not meet at evening
For death can take us unawares
So with generous hugs and kisses
We shake off those worldly cares

At dusk before I lay my head down
I will squeeze and hold you tight
I will pray that God will give me
A kind word to say tonight

> A word spoken in due season how good it
> is. (Prv 15:23)

Break My Heart

I want to be broken in heart and mind
I want You to break even my soul
Not by the things that matter to me
From those things I selfishly hold

Break me, Lord, in new ways
From things only important to me
I focus on temporal and earthly things
Not on the things as You feel and see

I focus on comfort and ease of my life
Things of my own personal concern
To be well liked and thought of as nice
As if the world around me must turn

Break my heart, Savior dear, my Lord
Give me the same pain that You feel
If I am truly to be called by Your name
If my faith is true and for real

I know what really matters in life
Make me count self as something that's lost
It is Your peace that I seek and Your joy that I want
Breaking my will is well worth the cost

> I want to know Christ and the power of his
> resurrection and the fellowship of sharing in his
> sufferings, becoming like him in his death, and
> so, somehow, to attain to the resurrection from
> the dead. (Phil 3:10–11)

Not Bright

Service, not science
Broken, not bright
Foolish, not facile
Leads people to light

In losing there is learning
In failing I am sure
There is much to be gained
In not finding the cure

For there may be no answers
The future may truly be bleak
But God gets great glory
When I admit that I am weak

So my model of helping
My methods of healing
Mean the least when I am standing
And the most when I am kneeling

> Because the foolishness of God is wiser than
> men and the weakness of God is stronger than
> men. (1 Cor 1:25)

Buy God a Watch

I am buying God a watch
To help Him keep better time
He shows up when He wants to
His concerns do not seem to match mine

I have a list of questions
A short list of demands
He seems so disinterested
I want to know where He stands

So I have decided the Almighty
Must have overslept
He has given me some promises
I expect them to be kept

So, dear Father, let's do this
Our watches synchronize
I will send up prayer requests
Just as You open Your eyes
It is not that I am in a hurry

But I am indeed finite
I have lots of stuff to do
So I will send my list tonight
By tomorrow, if You are not busy

Read my lists and grant my requests
It is a long list, so do not get dizzy
When You are finished, then You can rest

Ye ask, and receive not, because ye ask amiss, that ye may consume it upon your lusts. (James 4:3)

For a thousand years in your sight are like a day that has just gone by, or like a watch in the night. (Ps 90:4)

Careful Spending

I carefully measure the money I share
I don't want my cupboards to ever go bare
I could actually give more
But there are so many poor
After all Jesus said, "They would always be there"

I even measure the mercy I show
Being quite kind to those I love and I know
But if you cross my path
You will sure know my wrath
God's up there; I am in charge down below!

I dole out my pity with pride
Take a picture and get my good side
I am sharing my wealth
But I will not risk my own health
Now let us go shopping on the high side

I dole out the small coins I disperse
Way down deep in my pockets and purse
I am sure they can live
On the tidbits and scraps that I give
After all, without me it would be worse

> He which soweth sparingly shall reap sparingly, and he which soweth bountifully shall also reap bountifully. (2 Cor 9:6)

Come and Eat

Come sit with Me at My table
It is set with good bread and good meat
Let Me show you that I am still able
Let us sit down; let us share; let us eat

To serve you gives Me great pleasure
So let Me wash your hands, head, and feet
You are My Father's great treasure
Sit down, My dear child, and let us eat

The table that is now set before us
Costs My blood for your reserved seat
I conquered hell, Satan, and death's dust
Come, dear child, sit down and let us eat

Come sup with Me and My Father
The Holy Spirit does invite and entreat
The world says you are unworthy—do not bother
I bid you come sit down, and let us eat

This meal will change you to be just like Me
It will make even life's bitter things sweet
You will become what My Father says you should be
Come sit down, My dear child, and let us eat

> Here I am! I stand at the door and knock.
> If anyone hears my voice, and opens the door, I
> will come in and eat with him, and he with me.
> (Rv 3:20)

Damaged Goods

These were damaged goods
Full of canker and rust
No right mind would
Even wipe off the dust

To purchase such items
Out of date, out of style
We would rather look down
The higher-priced aisle

However, Jesus shopped
Among things cast away
For people deemed unworthy
In our high-fashioned day

He found me in a trash bin
Headed for the garbage heap
Instead He decided
That I was well worth to keep

He embraced me and then cleaned me
He changed my price tag
He washed me with a cloth
With His blood on the rag

As people look now
They never know where I have been
I was once damaged goods
Cleansed by Jesus from sin

I am worthy of heaven
I am of infinite worth
All because the great Master
Made His inventory on earth

> But God has chosen the foolish things of
> the world to confound the wise; and God have
> chosen the weak things of the world to confound
> the things which are mighty. 1 Cor 1:27

Did It in the Dark

I stood in the dark, and I hid it
In the shadows it was easy to hide
Only God and I know I did it
To all others I plainly just lied

It is the absence of good that is fearful
And without God there cannot be good
No matter how remorseful and tearful
I fear judgment when I don't do as I should

For as I do right, I have nothing to dread
Living holy I stand proud and erect
I could do wrong, but I do right instead
And the goodness of God does protect

Hell starts in my life right here
And heaven is just as close at hand
My Jesus has promised to be near
To lead me to that sweet promised land

If there is no good in the essence
Then there is no God at the source
If I am hiding my acts from His presence
I will reap pain and continued remorse

> For every one that does evil hates the light,
> and will not come into the light for fear that his
> deeds will be exposed.
> But whoever lives by the truth comes into
> the light, so that it may be seen plainly that what
> he has done has been done though God. (Jn
> 3:20–21)

Fall Asleep in My Arms

Fall asleep in My arms, My sweet loved one
Fall asleep and just let your mind rest
Leave your questions and troubles to Me only
Lay your head near My heart, on My breast

I will give comfort and a tender caress
I will keep you from all danger and harm
No harsh critique nor angry redress
Just come close be gathered in My arms

I find your soul of infinite value and worth
I shelter you with My comfort, My shield
For I was charged with death from the day of My birth
And it cost me My life—will you now yield?

Your own struggle further traps and ensnares
Depriving you of peace only I can provide
Like a babe that is restless with cares
You will find rest when by Me you abide

I will keep you from those who would use you
To awaken you with soft appeal but sure alarms
For the world surely wants to abuse you
Come to Me and fall asleep in My arms

> Come to me, all you who are weary and
> burdened, and I will give you rest. Take my yoke
> upon you and learn of me, for I am gentle and
> humble in heart: and you will find rest for your
> souls. (Mt 11:28–29)

Far Beyond

Far beyond what I deserved
So much more than I expected
My God has richly blessed me
I should have been rejected

Just the manner of my thoughts
Let alone my sinful deeds
I should now be in hell
Reap my crop from evil seeds

But my God, so rich in mercy
So abundant in His grace
Looked beyond my wicked past
And my wickedness erased

Each day I stand in awe
His love bellows as does thunder
He looks beyond the man I am
Why He does it is a wonder

But He does it breath by breath
One heartbeat and then again
Beyond deserving or expecting
My Father delivers me from sin

> For by grace are ye saved through faith; and
> that not of yourselves: [it is] the gift of God:
> Not of works, lest any man should boast.
> (Eph 2:8–9)

Forgetful Father

He seems to have a defect
He seems to have a fault
I remind Him of my failures
Things that dominate my thoughts

But somehow He cannot recall
My sordid past of shame
He looks at His book of failures
But He does not see my name

I recall to Him my present
How I ruthlessly misuse
His favor and His grace
How His mercy I abuse

He turns to hosts of heaven
He looks down to the depths of hell
He searches earth beneath
He finds no one who can tell

For He tabulates and measures
He keeps eternal counts and weights
He returns with a final verdict
He tells me of my fate

He says to me
"Dear son, I do not find your sin
It appears the price was paid
You need not think on them again

"For I do keep perfect records
I do punish and do damn
But it appears your slate was cleaned
By the One Who said 'I am'"

So when anyone reminds you
Of your failings and your falls
Tell them you have a merciful Father
He has forgiven and forgotten all

If it no longer bothers Him
When your past comes back to you
When reminded by accusers
Take your forgetful Father's view

For I will forgive their wickedness and will
remember their sins no more. (Heb 8:12)

God's Party Tricks

I know You can do this, Lord
I read it in Your Book
You have that certain power
You create with just a look

So I am going to ask this once
I will not revisit this again
Just let me hit the lotto
Give me a chance to win

You parted the Red Sea
You brought water from a rock
You made the blind man see
Raised Lazarus—what a shock

You made water turn to wine
Spit in a deaf man's ear
So if You are so inclined
Let me make this request clear

If You let me hit the number
I will give You half of all I win
You can do with it what You want
You just allow me to freely spend

If You do not think You are able
If this is too big a stunt
Just do like we do in football
Do not pass; do not run; just punt

I will settle for half the winnings
Do not need the whole jackpot
After all You do not need Your half
So I will not put You on the spot

> And he said, "This will I do. I will pull
> down my barns and build greater and there will
> I bestow all my fruits and my goods." (Lk 12:18)

Growing My Grudges

I plant each grudge seed with care
I make sure to give plenty of space
Each plant needs plenty of air
I delete any pretense of grace

Grace only inhibits the growth in soil
It will not allow the seedlings to sprout
Mercy only makes grudges spoil
So like weeds, I pull them both out

At the harvest I have plenty to show
Though nothing that can feed or make well
But the grudges are in a nice row
Take a taste and experience hell

I know my garden serves no godly reason
It does not help, heal, or even make whole
And at the end of each planting season
I lose a little bit more of my soul

I had better let Jesus tend my small garden
It would be best to let Him till the ground
The fruit that He grows is sin's pardon
And life forever in Him is found

> Wherefore by their fruits you shall know them. (Mt 7:20)
> Abide in me and I in you. As the branch cannot bear fruit of itself, except it abide in the vine, no more can you, except you abide in me. (Jn 15:4)

Help Me to Die

Help me die with You, Lord
Help me die by Your side
For I know I'll be rewarded
With the loss of my self-seeking pride

My pride and my lust
Bring me heartache and pain
To obey You in trust
Is true life and true gain

But I fear what men say
They will think I am weak
As I learn to obey
They will ill of me speak

They will call me a fool
Say I trust in "some god"
That religion is a tool
Makes me look stupid and odd

I fear I may lose
The friends I hold near
If it is You Whom I choose
I lose what seems dear

So You must help me to die
You must help me decide
Dry my eyes as I cry
This is not suicide

Give me strength to commit
Give me strength to obey
Give me strength to submit
To Your will and Your way

> Then Paul answered, "Why are your weep-
> ing and breaking my heart? I am ready not only
> to be bound, but also to die in Jerusalem for the
> name of the Lord Jesus." (Acts 21:13)

I Hid in My Bed

I hid in my bed
And covered my head
Trying hard to forget what I did
Or what I said

So I lay there real still
Just trying to "chill"
Hoping with time
All else would be fine

The world kept on spinning
The sun rose and set
Right from the beginning
No one knew I was upset

So I decided to get up
Get back in the ring
Though I had laid a low blow
I could still make a fair swing

Forgiving myself
Is the toughest thing yet
Moving on to tomorrow
Learning how to forget

So get out from the covers
Open the blinds and the shades
God wants you to know
You are wonderfully made

You are His beloved
He still gives you breath
There is no need to covet
No need to fear death

Enjoy the sun's rays
Enjoy the moon's glow
As the Bible still says
Your God loves you so

> Nor height nor depth nor any creature shall
> be able to separate us from the love of God which
> is in Christ Jesus our Lord. (Rom 8:39)

I Hid in the Shadows

I hid in the shadows
When You called my name
I heard Your voice calling
But I was ashamed

Have you done what I told you?
Have you done what I asked?
Have you finished your duties?
Have you completed the task?

Oh, Lord, You know all
You know I have failed
So I am hiding from You
For I could not prevail

The temptations were great
It was easy to sin
I found out too late
I had just given in

So I hid as did Adam
When he made the wrong choice
I knew You were calling
I heard Your strong voice

Full of fear and foreboding
For the consequent pain
Fear of chastisement and scolding
For not revering Your name

Then You bade me, "Dear son
I knew you would fall
That is why I was searching
When you heard me call

"I want to provide you
With all that you need
To welcome you home
To see you succeed

"When I call your name
When I speak to your heart
Don't run in shame
It only tears you apart

"I will clothe you again
Not with the coverings of skin
As Adam my firstborn
Used to cover his sin

"I will cover your body
Your naked, cold, shivering frame
No need to hide in the shadows
Your garment is Christ Jesus by name"

> Today, if you will hear his voice, do not harden your hearts. (Heb 4:7)

I Went Dark on Jesus

I had no problem with Him
When He made my mama well
He was well within His rights
'Till He started talking about hell

I could welcome His sweet blessings
Of prosperity and wealth
But He started to go messing
With how my habits hurt my health

So I decided I would filter
And decipher parts I liked
If His attitude was out of kilter
I would tell Him to take a hike

I would pretend I had lost reception
That my set was on the blink
I would not allow connection
Stay in the dark so I could think

How I could stay outside His radar
Hide from His wide sweep and search
After all there are lots of places
Unexplored on this big earth

But the more I chose the darkness
The closer He would come
He extended His hand toward me
And said, "Come home, My son"

I had to give up hiding
From His great and awesome power
Because He never stops abiding
With me every minute, every hour

> If they ascend up into heaven, thou art
> there: if I make my bed in hell behold thou art
> there. (Ps 39:8)

I Would Rather Be Lonely

I would rather be lonely than love You
I would rather spend life with despise
For to love You is to want Your approval
And I feel good enough in my own eyes

I would rather spend life on my own terms
I would rather not have You decide
What is right, what is wrong, right, or left
I can't by Your decisions abide

For to love You and follow Your commandments
Is to admit that I don't know the way
And my ego cannot understand it
I don't want to do as You say

I would rather spend eternity elsewhere
If it means submitting to what You say is true
If there is only one way to heaven
I do not want it if that way is You

Such is the thought of my flesh
As I wrestle with submission to Christ
Each day this fight is afresh
To admit that He paid the price

My angry and unforgiving spirit
My selfish and lustful desires
I must relinquish if I truly love Jesus
And only He can extinguish these fires

So if it means that I truly want heaven
Then I must give Him total control
For the Father sent Him to save me
And to sanctify my body and soul

If I don't want loneliness and sorrow
If I truly want life at its best
I must give my all today, not tomorrow
And, like a child, lay my head on His breast

> If you love me, you will keep what I command. (Jn 14:15)
>
> If you obey my commandments, you will remain in my love, just as I have obeyed my Father's commands and remain in his love. (Jn 15:10)

Loosen My Belt

I loosen my belt
I untie my shoes
I am completely at home
I am alone just with you

I close every curtain
Shut every door tight
I want to be certain
No disturbance tonight

You place your hand on my shoulder
I place my head on your breast
Your love has made me grow bolder
Your love gives me true rest

We sleep together until morning
You awaken me with a smile
Your love has made me refreshed
What I needed all the while

As I prepare for the day
Open windows and open blinds
I hear you speak clearly
To my heart and my mind

Throughout the day I will be with you
Call my name; hold my hand
There will be challenges and trials
Things you will not understand

You will face many struggles
And you may feel alone
Bring all your day's troubles
To me back at home

Tonight, give me your fears
Tonight, give me your pain
Your failures, your tears
Give them to me once again

I will be here to give comfort
I will be here to provide
We can rest here together
Come, dearest love; come close by my side

> Draw near to God, and he will draw near to
> you. (Jas 4:8)

My Enemy's Pain

I take no joy in my enemy's trouble
Though he may take much joy in mine
To repay him with evil seems to make sense
But to forgive him like Jesus is divine

Though my enemy seeks to defame and destroy
My call is to build up and forgive
By human standards I seem like a fool
But that is how Jesus commands me to live

When he who hates me is hungry and feeling great thirst
It makes sense to let him die in his pain
But if I am truly putting my trust in Jesus first
I must forgive him again and again

I must give water to relieve his parched tongue
I must feed him to help him gain strength
I must not recall to him the wrong he has done
Be prepared to go to any length

To save my enemy from what I feel he deserves
Is the only righteous thing I can do
For if it is truly Christ Jesus I serve
I must believe that what He says is all true

Jesus told me that if I would be forgiven
I must not forgiveness withhold
I pray that it is with mercy I am driven
And God's mercy will help make me bold

Bold enough to forgive and bold enough to obey
Bold enough to give mercy without measure
Bold enough to stand before God the last day
To forgive gives my Father great pleasure

For He forgave me and never seems to tire of this
He forgives when I will not even confess
So if I claim to know Him and cannot forgive
I have failed this most simple test

For I cannot know Him or claim to be His
If I seek revenge and harbor ill thought
For it is not my enemy who is measured in this
This is what my Master has taught

> For if you forgive men their sin against you,
> your heavenly Father will also forgive you,
> But if you do not forgive men their sins, your
> Father will not forgive your sins. (Mt 6:14–15)

My Lover Called

My Lover called me last night
He said, "I have been trying to reach you
You have been out of range, out of sight."
I said, "I have so much to do.

"I am busy with work and my studies
My favorite shows on TV
Then I have to hang with my buddies
And last of all, there's downtime with me

"So You see, dear Lover, do not be offended
I will call You when I need You here
Just wait 'till this TV series ended
Give me time, Lover; please try to be fair"

My Lover paused for a moment
He was quiet and as usual polite
He said, "Indeed I will not rush you
I do know your schedule is tight

"Just remember that if you let Me get closer
If you give Me more time and more prayer
You will find all distractions and troubles
Will disappear with your woes and your cares

"For I am a lover, understanding and patient
I do not rush in without invitation
When you realize you are lonely without Me
I will meet you in all situations

"But as long as you feel you don't need Me
I will let you go your way as you will
Just remember I am here waiting for you
For My love is both eternal and real"

> Behold, I stand at the door, and knock if
> any man hear my voice, and open the door, I will
> come in to him, and will sup with him, and he
> with me. (Rv 3:20)

Never Forgive You

I will never forgive you
Because you never forgave
You wanted revenge
I wanted to save

You nursed your hurt feelings
You rehearsed every pain
I wanted to heal you
You refused time and again

Your wounded emotions
Your painful reflection
Your great disappointments
That sense of rejection

You continue to judge
To feel hurt and disgust
You now justify
This complete lack of trust

So if you never forgive
And you never forget
My word on this subject
Is what you give you will get

> For if you forgive men when they sin against
> you, your heavenly Father will also forgive you.
> But if you do not forgive men their sins, your
> Father will not forgive your sins. (Mt 6:14–15)

Never Gets Easy

Her face was swollen
Her eyes tearstained
I tried to hurry out
To avoid looking again

Her illness so advanced
Her body deformed
Full of sores, bleeding wounds
My own heart was torn

I spoke in soft tones
She stared in disbelief
"I can offer you nothing
No, there is no relief

"You will die very soon
No matter that you are young
And since you cannot afford payments
There is less to be done"

Having finished my speech
Having hardened my heart
I quickly ran to the door
Hoping she would depart

But she sat there just staring
Did not budge, would not move
I returned, prayed with her
For peace and strength from above

She finally left still in tears
Still in grief and in pain
The scenario of bad news
I do it time and again

It never gets easy
It never seems right
I take this burden to Jesus
With Him, it gets light

Come unto me, all you who are weary and
burdened, and I will give you rest. For my yoke is
easy and my burden is light. (Mt 11:28, 30)

No Rest for You

I will never let you know comfort
I will never let you know rest
I will never let you have joy
Until you give Me your best

Oh, the world will settle for seconds
It sets expectations real low
It lets you choose fashion and pleasure
None for substance, only for show

But I have greater demands
I expect much more from you
You are My creation
I have great works that you must do

I call upon you to surrender
To subject yourself to My way
You can choose your own way, but remember
I alone can keep death far away

If you really want all that is good
If you desire to have the best of it all
Heed My voice, My commands, and My statutes
Come to Me, dearest child, and heed My call

> For forty years I was angry with that generation; I said, "They are a people whose hearts go astray, and they have not known my ways. I decided on oath in my anger, 'They shall never enter my rest.'" (Ps 95:10–11)

Out of the Closet

I am coming out the closet this year
I refuse to live in constant fear
That others will know that I lay claim
To that great and marvelously holy name

I will no longer pretend to be another good guy
Just praying enough to look good and get by
It will no longer bother me who knows or sees
If I fold my hands or bend my knees

I refuse to act "religious" and pretend
Worried about whom I impress or offend
I will live out my faith as though seen by God alone
Coming out of the closet, knowing His blood did atone

> If anyone is ashamed of me and my words
> in this adulterous and sinful generation, the Son
> of Man will be ashamed of him when he comes
> in his Father's glory with the holy angels. (Mk
> 8:38)

Resolution

I do not want your resolutions
I already know where you stand
I am the ultimate solution
Just do what I command

If you will only just surrender
Just give in and do as I say
My love is surreal and so tender
But things must be done My way

The new promises you make are not lasting
They vanish the moment you encounter new stress
Things like diet, without even fasting
Before the first night falls, you will have failed this first test

You believe you can stop lustful behavior
Yet you watch and listen to soft porn
You neglect to meditate on the Savior
You miss the whole purpose for which He was born

Your old disputes and grudges you still treasure
Though you promised to make that phone call
It seems being hurt gives you pleasure
So this will once again stall

Just let go of these matters of trifle
You cannot change you, so do not try to pretend
For you do not have the power to stifle
Each year has proven; just look at your last end

Do not resolve to be the best that you can be
It falls so short of whom I can make of you
Surrender, submit, and obey Me
No resolutions, instead I will make you brand-new

> Therefore, if anyone is in Christ, he is a new creation; the old has gone, the new has come! (2 Cor 5:17)

Only One Way Out

Of this there is no question
Of this there is no doubt
When it comes to leaving this life
There's only one way out

You can try the newest therapy
You can chant and scream and shout
Use magic potions, oils, and such
There is still only one way out

You can cry and plead for mercy
You can pray petition and pout
But just like all before you
There is only one way out

So get in line like all the others
Who discovered what life's about
Either heaven or hell awaits you
And there's only one way out

> Jesus saith unto him, I am the way, the truth, and the life: no man cometh unto the Father, but by me. (Jn 14:6 KJV)

Send Someone

Send someone my way, Lord
Someone who needs a smile
Someone who has deep sorrow
Who has not known joy awhile

Send them my way for comfort
Send them my way for peace
Let me be the vessel
Through whom Your joy is released

Let them find Your spirit in me
Let them see Your lovely face
And as You use my voice and hands
Their fears and pain erase

Yes, do send them my way, Lord
Or if must be then send me there
They may not have the courage
Their needs and burdens to share

As You use me to heal and touch
Your grace through me will flow
I will also be renewed and filled
As my faith in You does grow

I am willing to be used
To show anyone in need
That You can defeat all troubles
Please send, Lord; I will heed

> Then I heard the voice of the Lord saying,
> "Whom shall I send? And who will go for us?"
> And I said, "Here am I; send me." (Is 6:8)

So Safe, So Warm

There is nothing like a rainy day
That is filled with cold and wind
That makes me want to stay inside
And spend more time with Him

He seems to always have the time
To sit and talk and share
It is just that I am so busy
I hardly know He is there

And yet when I do need Him
He never says, "Not now"
He makes the time and takes the time
I don't know why or how

I do know that He loves me
It feels so safe and warm
To know that He is above me
And yet I am in His arms

So safe and warm inside
Yet outside cold winds blow
It is time with Him alone, aside
True peace and comfort I know

> Never will I leave you; Never will I forsake
> you. (Heb 13:5)

Surrender to Me

I will be found
When you are meek
Not when you are strong
But when you are weak

You see My sweet love
You still want your way
You ignore, even scorn
The words that I say

Your perceived self-reliance
Your deluded self-defense
Is just pure defiance
It has no logic or sense

You have no real resource
That comes not from Me
Your only safe recourse
Is to admit and then see

It is I alone Who daily provide
It is I alone Who truly do care
Everywhere that you hide
I am standing right there

Just surrender your will
Please surrender your strength
I am waiting still
I will go any length

I would die for you
In fact, I did this, you see
Now that is love that is true
Now go live for Me!

> If I go up to the heavens, you are there; if
> I make my bed in the depths, you are there. (Ps
> 139:8)

The Gift I Want Is You

You search for deals
You search for sales
While all I want
Is that My love prevails

You think I am pleased
By how much you spend
But without true love
All your gifts just offend

I do not want jewels
I certainly do not need clothes
I cannot use perfume
You can keep all those

Give Me your heart
Give Me yourself
All the other stuff
Can stay on the shelf

To celebrate Me
Do not focus on you
For I am all that is good
I am all that is true

> He hath shewed thee, O man, what is good;
> and what doth the Lord require of thee, but to do
> justly, and to love mercy, and walk humbly with
> thy God? (Mi 6:8)

The Other Cheek

If it is peace that I want
If it is joy that I seek
I will find it only
When I offer my cheek

For it is not in revenge
That is the mark of the weak
But true strength is shown
When I offer my cheek

I cannot find God's best
Unless like Jesus I am meek
I find my Father's favor
When I offer my cheek

In the valley of self-pity
From anger's mountain peak
I can do no harm to others
When I offer my cheek

"Find true rest, dearest child"
Here Jesus does speak
If you claim to be His
You must offer your cheek

> But I tell you, do not resist an evil person. If someone strikes you on the right cheek, turn to him the other also. (Mt 5:39)

Magic Prayer

I raised my hand
I bowed my head
And then these
Magic words I said

"Lord, come and live
Inside of me
And from the evil
Please set me free

"In Jesus's name"
I said this prayer
And then I hurried
Out of there

"Boy, that was close"
I said to self
I almost became like
Someone else

Why should I change?
I'm pretty good
I'll just use Jesus
As I should

As a cover for
The possible case
That God will judge
The human race

And since He heard
My speech just then
He'll overlook
My life of sin

I'll live my life
Just as I want
That hell He mentioned
Is just a taunt

And so it is
That many a sinner
Will go to hell
Believing they're a winner

> Not every one that saith unto me, Lord, Lord, shall enter into the kingdom of heaven; but he that doeth the will of my Father which is in heaven. (Mt 7:21 KJV)

Have It Your Way

You take pride in exerting your will
Instead of submitting to Mine
So the emptiness that you now feel
Is because you ignore the divine

You take pleasure in having your way
In getting in the last word
Making sure they hear what you say
If you were silent, it is Me they'd have heard

You plant seeds of what you call fruit
You water and watch over with care
But your harvest is all self-pursuit
You neglect self-denial and prayer

Take control if you want; I won't deny it
I won't force you into submission
Run your life as you will; go on try it
I only enter your life with permission

> There is a way *that seems* right to a man,
> But its end *is* the way of death. (Prv 14:12
> New King James Version [NKJV])
> Behold, I stand at the door, and knock: if any man hear my voice, and open the door, I will come in to him, and will sup with him, and he with me. (Rv 3:20 KJV)

Take Him for Granted

He is someone I take for granted
I don't even consider He's there
However, when things fall apart
It is only then that my problems I share

For my Father has never forsaken
He has never denied me His time
But I know without question or forethought
I am too busy to share some of mine

So I walk through life self-assured
Knowing that somehow I'll make it through
And if I do have a problem I will call Him
Until then, I've got my own things to do

This relationship is clearly lopsided
It favors my agenda and plans
I am ashamed to admit that my failures
Are from times I ignored His commands

Today I vow to no longer take Him for granted
I will seek the Father's presence and grace
I pray, "Holy Spirit, please guide me
Help me seek my God face-to-face"

> I love them that love me; and those that
> seek me early shall find me. (Prv 8:17)

The Same Every Year

Every year you do the same
You celebrate Christmas
But you do not mention My name

You drape your home with cheap tinsel and foil
It makes you feel good
But you forget I am royal

You stand in long lines buying lots of new stuff
You say it is in My honor
Well, I have had enough

Do something for Me this holiday season
Reflect on My birth
It was for a real reason

> Your new moons and your appointed feasts
> my soul hate it: they are a trouble unto me; I am
> weary to bear them. (Is 1:14)

The Same Stuff

The same stuff I promised God before
I will promise Him again
I make the same old pledges
I make at each year's end

I promise I will watch my weight
I will not cuss anymore
I will stop my smoking and my drinking
I will finish all my chores

I will read my Bible and pray more often
I will go to church each week
I will be more careful about movies I watch
I will be careful how I speak

I will greet the folks I do not like
With genuine smiles and greetings
I will give my best to charities
I will be on time for meetings

In fact, I will remind my God
Last year what I had promised Him I would do
And if He had remembered then
Then I would remember too

With each New Year's resolution
I revisit my situation
And most often find my present promise
Was last year's destination

The change I desire greatly
The change I desperately crave
Can only be accomplished
By accepting that God saves

And unless I release the old stuff
The same stuff that I hold
Next year I will make the same promises
I will be the me of old

> Create in me a pure heart, O God, and
> renew a steadfast spirit within me. (Ps 51:10)

This Time I Travel Naked

The things I treasure most
Are the things I leave behind
The things of greatest worth
Should really occupy my mind

But the things I fear to part with
Are the things I cannot keep
Oh my, the mere denial
Causes the flesh in me to weep

The life of pleasure and of plenty
Life of ease and choice and such
The mere thought of no selection
Puts my mind in a state of flux

I must get used to smaller menus
To accommodate single toppings
No variety of venues
No streetlights and, yes, no stopping

I leave the world of many trappings
Returning lighter than I arrived
I travel lighter; yes, it feels naked
Unclothed of greed, envy, and pride

Being home God has reordered
Both my wardrobe and my gear
He has reminded me to pack lightly
For my eternity's not here

I will travel with the clothes He gives me
In His fashions there's no waste
It all fits well, shows He forgives me
Shows the world God has good taste

For we brought nothing into this world and
it is certain we can carry nothing out. (1 Tm 6:7)

If You'd Prayed

Imagine the difference
It would have made
Instead of arguing
If you had prayed

Imagine the influence
If on knees you stayed
Instead of standing
You knelt down and prayed

Imagine the impact
You could have displayed
Instead of demanding
You bowed your head and prayed

I'd open the flood gates
I'd let bad memories fade
Instead of being bitter
Sweetness comes when you pray

> If my people, which are called by my name,
> shall humble themselves, and pray, and seek my
> face, and turn from their wicked ways; then will I
> hear from heaven, and will forgive their sin, and
> will heal their land. (2 Chr 7:14)

I Make You God!

You occupy my every thought
You are emblazoned on my mind
When I eat and drink, I think of you
You are a god of a different kind

My mood, my habits revolve around you
When you are near, I find great peace
If you turn your back or hide your face
My joy and happiness cease

Though I know you did not create me
And I know you don't sustain
My mind still revolves around you
I crave to hear your name

I have made you my god
It is you I worship and adore
You define my character and person
It is you I truly live for

Such is my search for truth
I look to fashion and my friends
To find who I am meant to be
It all leads to dead ends

I will only find true joy
When I cease from selfish aim
When I find the God of life
When I take on my Father's name

For whoso findeth me findeth life, and shall obtain favour of the LORD.

But he that sinneth against me wrongeth his own soul: *all they that hate me love death.* (Prv 8:35–36, emphasis added)

You Are My Best

With all the world within My hands
Every living being at My command
I chose you as a gift to earth
You are a treasure of eternal worth

The moon and stars now common signs
For thousands of years they marked the times
The winds and waves moved to and fro
Mere whims of mine, My will to show

The snow, the rain, the nights and days
My most simple thoughts to show My ways
The angels watch with bated breath
To see Me put My own self to test

Could I create a more glorious thing
Than they themselves My praise to sing?
Then I revealed my greatest plan
A being like Me, I called it man

The wonder of this special one
Would be that I could call him son
And unlike anything else I'd make
He could choose to go or choose to stay

Praise is your chance; it is your choice
You can praise or curse Me with your voice
Remember that I made you free
And no other creature has that right, you see

You are the summit of My creation
The universe meets at this summation
To wait and see if My own will claim
To inherit and embrace My holy name

You are and have the best
Claim it in Me and in Me alone

> Behold, what manner of love the Father hath bestowed upon us, that we should be called the sons of God: therefore the world knoweth us not, because it knew him not.
>
> Beloved, now are we the sons of God, and it doth not yet appear what we shall be: but we know that, when he shall appear, we shall be like him; for we shall see him as he is. (1 Jn 3:1–2)

Your Doormat

Make me your doormat
To serve in surrender
No display for myself
Let me point to Your splendor

As people come near
Help them step over and up
Let them ignore me as they come
Let them drink from Your cup

May they ignore, even smear, me
So they can see only You
I'm the doormat, not the door
You are all that is true

Lord, make them feel welcome
Use me to point the way
As a doormat, not the doorbell
Help me submit and obey

> According to my earnest expectation and my hope, that in nothing I shall be ashamed, but that with all boldness, as always, so now also Christ shall be magnified in my body, whether it be by life, or by death. For to me to live is Christ, and to die is gain. (Phil 1:20–21)

Pimples and Dimples

My Lover keeps it simple
My Lover makes it plain
My Lover knows my laugh
My Lover knows my pain

He knows I'm far from perfect
Even when I try my best
He focuses on my good points
And de-emphasize the rest

My Lover kisses pimples
Those on the cheeks and nose
Just as He smooches dimples
Because my Lover knows

The pimples are a part of me
Their marks etched into my face
But my dimples will fade with time
Leaving wrinkles in their trace

So my Lover chooses both
That is His preference, you see
Failures, faults, and foibles
This is why my Lover chooses me

For if He saw only dimples
And as those sweet traits do leave
His love in turn would grow cold
That would cause my heart to grieve

So He kisses every pimple
Every blackhead, scar, and mole
That is love, true love indeed
My Lover satisfies my soul

> For HE knows OUR frame; HE remembers that we dust. (Ps 103:14)
> You don't have a soul; you have a body. You are a soul. (C. S. Lewis)

You Won't See Me

It may seem rather biased
You may call Me unfair
But if you didn't see Me down here
You won't see Me up there

Oh, I know you went to church
Gave some money, your good share
But if you didn't see Me down here
You won't see Me up there

You sang in choir and ushered
You taught Sunday school with care
Even preached and gave out Bibles
That won't mean you'll see Me there

You somehow overlooked Me
When I was hungry, sick, and bare
So since you did not see Me down here
You won't see Me up there

You neglected Me in prison
Didn't seem to know or care
So since you did not see Me down here
You won't see Me up there

I was hungry, thirsty, lonely
Begging for someone to share
You stepped over; you ignored Me
No, you won't see Me up there

For if you really want to praise Me
Don't stand looking up in the air
I am here; I walk among you
Serve Me here, and then see Me there

> Then shall they also answer him, saying,
> Lord, when saw we thee an hungred, or athirst,
> or a stranger, or naked, or sick, or in prison, and
> did not minister unto thee?
>
> Then shall he answer them, saying, Verily I
> say unto you, Inasmuch as ye did it not to one of
> the least of these, ye did it not to me. And these
> shall go away into everlasting punishment: but
> the righteous into life eternal. (Mt 25:44–46)

Band-Aid on Cancer

I put a Band-Aid on his cancer
I fed his hunger with a pill
I ignored the circumstances
That had really made him ill

I looked deep in my black bag
Stethoscope and BP cuff
I assured him that in one week
My quick fix would be enough

I then took pictures of my doings
All good deeds must be recorded
When he asked, "How much your camera?"
I said, "You can't afford it!"

Then I bundled my belongings
Left behind unwanted clothing
Back to my air-conditioned flight home
Full of self, full of loathing

Loathing the sights I again witnessed
Knowing his pill would wear off that night
His cancer grew; his hunger increased
I was safe, away in flight

Do you too put Band-Aids on cancers?
Do you write the checks and then sigh?
How on earth it got so bad?
Well, you are part the reason why

For if you and I avoid the tumors
The wretched, filthy, destitute
We are both part of the blame
This truth we can't refute

Give, go, or send is the commandment
That our God has long declared
Stop the quick and easy fixes
Don't pretend I really care

Stop the pills and stop the potions
Short-term, simple, cute, quaint answers
Lord, when did I see You?
He answered, "You put a Band-Aid on My cancers"

> And the King shall answer and say unto them, Verily I say unto you, Inasmuch as ye have done it unto one of the least of these my brethren, ye have done it unto me. (Mt 25:40)
>
> Is not this the fast that I have chosen? to loose the bands of wickedness, to undo the heavy burdens, and to let the oppressed go free, and that you break every yoke? Is it not to deal thy bread to the hungry, and that you bring the poor that are cast out to your house? when you see the naked, that thou cover him; and that you hide not yourself from your own flesh?
>
> And if you draw out your soul to the hungry, and satisfy the afflicted soul; then shall your light rise in obscurity, and your darkness be as the noonday. (Is 58:6–7, 10)

Feeding on Froth

I prefer to voice my disdain
To make all know my pain
I feed on my own sorrows
Feels good when I complain

I feed on my own spittle
I choke on what is little
When the feast is all around me
I chew on what is brittle

As a dying man's death throttle
I collect my froth in bottle
When others come with struggles
I share with them these "bubbles"

So forgive me when I spit
Self-serving is my name
Feed on froth not satisfying
But it gives me cause to blame

God, forgive me for my choking
Fixing things that are not broken
I confess my love for pity
My complaints make praise a token

> For I was envious at the foolish, when I saw
> the prosperity of the wicked. (Ps 73:3)

Deny Him

He knew that I would deny Him
Refuse to even acknowledge His name
Yet He loved and even embraced me
Though I held Him in contemptuous shame

When asked "Do you know Jesus?"
I held my tongue, silent, in fear
Who would notice or care that I claimed Him
Though He named me as precious and dear

Now I question; I wonder; I fret
Why did I hold Him in such awful reproach?
Then He holds His scarred hands toward me
He bids me come near and approach

Oh, the wonder of such love that embraces
Despite my refusal, my pride and self-interest
The Christ bids me—He even does beg me
Come close and lay my head on His breast

So even though I deny that I know Him
He will never deny whom He calls
He picks me up no matter how filthy
I am when I stumble and fall

> Come unto me all ye who labor and are
> heavy burden and I will give you rest. (Mt 11:28)
> He is despised and rejected of men; a man
> of sorrows, and acquainted with grief: and we hid
> as it were our faces from him; he was despised,
> and we esteemed him not. (Is 53:3)

Not Happy, Not Healthy, but Holy

Despite all the glow and the glamor
Despite all the noise, all the clamor
God wishes me not riches or fame
That does nothing to praise His good name

I seek what the world has to offer
Fill my bank, fill my financial coffer
But God wants to fill me with much more
And that is what He's waiting for

Oh, I know there are preachers who tell you
There are sermons that seek to compel you
To gain what you can in this life
Good husband, perfect home, perfect wife

But the God Whom I serve wants to fill me
With something that doesn't just thrill me
He has so much better in store
Than I could even ask for

He wants me to be perfect and holy
Not just happy and healthy solely
Because happy and healthy will perish
It is His holiness He wants me to cherish

Holiness is not it—it is Him
Not some wish, not some passing whim
It is what God has called me to be
Health and happiness will both soon flee

So I must seek His holiness always
And cherish it all my days
Health and happiness themselves not a sin
But they mean nothing if I don't have Him

> Then Simon Peter answered him, Lord, to
> whom shall we go? Thou hast the words of eter-
> nal life. (Jn 6:68)

Turn Invisible Moo into Meat

Only the Creator can do it
Only He can perform this feat
Make something from absolutely nothing
Turn invisible moo into meat

We can season and stir lightly
We can cook at just the right heat
Only He makes void become substance
Turn invisible moo into meat

He doesn't stop with one item
From cucumbers to red beet
Put *oink*, *swish*, and *cluck* on the menu
Turn invisible moo into meat

Evolutionists will shout and laugh at you
Their theories are lies and deceit
Black cow eats green grass, gets white milk
Because God turns invisible moo into meat

In the beginning God created the heaven and the earth and the earth was without form, and void; and darkness was upon the face of the deep. And the Spirit of God moved upon the face of the waters. And God said, Let there be light: and there was light. And God saw the light, that it was good: and God divided the light from the darkness. (Gn 1:1–4)

Through faith we understand that the worlds were framed by the word of God, so that things which are seen were not made of things which do appear. (Heb 11:3)

Break Them Again

If it brings You great glory
Though it may cause me great pain
Though all my bones be broken
Please break them once again

If it indeed makes me more holy
Though it may seem quite insane
If my bones and joints are crumbling
Please break them once again

If it helps others get their healing
If others will somehow gain
From my bones in trauma and turmoil
Please break them once again

My bones are in Your hands, Lord
They are marked with sin's deep stain
And since You alone mend them
Please break them once again

> Make me to hear joy and gladness; that the bones which thou hast broken may rejoice. (Ps 38:8)

Silly Poor Man

I walked out of the shoe store
And noticed his stark stare
Another silly poor man
Now what was he doing there?

He opened his dry lips
His teeth were cracked and brown
He asked me stupid questions
While I looked at the ground

"Why do you need two pairs?
And yet another tie?"
I answered him straightforward
I did not bat an eye

"While you look at me in awe
So unkempt and so disheveled
I choose to dress in splendor
And thus denounce the devil

I have exquisite fine tastes
For hats and suits and shoes
From the finest and the latest
Are the things I dare to choose

Besides you may not know this
That the gospel I have heard
Tells me I deserve this
It is written in God's Word

So you see, you silly poor man
You need to hear this gospel
Of great riches and great wealth
I am a faithful rich apostle"

And as I stepped away
This poor man grabbed my hand
He said, "Just wait a minute
You do not understand

"I am the Christ you claim
The Savior you confess
And you abuse My name
By boasting of how you dress

"You may continue in your pride
Seeking others to impress
Before death stops you in your stride
Seek Me now is what I suggest"

> But God said unto him, thou fool, this night
> thy soul shall be required of the: then whose shall
> those things be which thou has provided? (Lk
> 12:20)

Swallowing Time

Let the future swallow the present
And let the present digest the past
For the longer you hold on to what's wrong
The longer your pain still lasts

I alone am above time and eternity
I alone see all things as done
In your effort to win and get even
Restarts the fight I have already won

As you nurse the pain they have caused
As you continue to hold on to each grudge
You try to steal from My glory
I alone am defendant, lawyer, and judge

As you relive and rehearse each offense
As you try to get even or win
You negate and work against My plans
And that is what I call sin

I hold time and eternity and your now
I have appointed for your life each event
I do it because I am sovereign
I want you to rest on My strength

So, child, let go of the things that have hurt you
Embrace the very people you feel don't deserve
Let My grace dwell within you in all times
Let grace control each fiber and nerve

Forgiveness and grace are My virtues
And as I bestow My best upon you
Let go of the past and the present
See things from My point of view

As you ignore each tick of the clock
Allowing revenge and fear to control
You allow dangers of the past and the present
To conquer your spirit and soul

Make My future for you be your one aim
Let your hurts be swallowed with grace
Let the future with Me control all
Let your memory of times past be erased

> For if you forgive men their trespasses, your
> Heavenly Father will also forgive you. (Mt 6:14)

My Enemies' Peace

Lord, give my enemies peace
Let their smiles and laughter increase
May they know ever-increasing strength
To their life days add great length
May their joy and comfort never cease

Lord, use their wealth as distraction
Let them know only sweet satisfaction
So that when I come to their mind
They only have energy and time
To pursue peace as the best course of action

> But to you who are listening I say: Love your enemies, do good to those who hate you. (Lk 6:27)
>
> But love your enemies, do good to them, and lend to them without expecting to get anything back. Then your reward will be great, and you will be children of the Most High, because he is kind to the ungrateful and wicked. (Lk 6:35)

The Vine

"Look at all my beautiful branches
How the tentacles intertwine"
He said, "Because there is no fruit
I have to cut this piece of vine"

"But, Lord, they are so beautiful
I am sure we will get wine"
He said, "Not from leaves and branches
I must prune this pretty vine"

"But, Lord, it's so attractive
And people know this branch is mine"
He picked up the sheers and scissors
And cut my favorite piece of vine

I told him, "Lord, You hurt me
Down to my core into my spine"
He continued to inspect
Looking for fruit, not leafy vine

And daily He surveys my life
Knowing what He expects to find
And though the results may please me
I am just a branch; He is the Vine

I must let repent of ego
Pride and self-pleasure cross the line
Yield, submit, and, yes, surrender
Fruit comes only when abiding in the Vine

I am the true vine, and my Father is the husbandman.

Every branch in me that beareth not fruit he taketh away: and every branch that beareth fruit, he purgeth it, that it may bring forth more fruit. Abide in me, and I in you. As the branch cannot bear fruit of itself, except it abide in the vine; no more can ye, except ye abide in me. I am the vine, ye are the branches: He that abideth in me, and I in him, the same bringeth forth much fruit: for without me ye can do nothing. (Jn 15:1–2, 4–5)

The Best You Can Do?

I go to bed each night
With a simplistic point of view
Lord, I didn't get my way today
Is that the best that You can do?

I wanted a bigger car
I wanted a nicer house too
After all everyone else has it
Is that the best that You can do?

I want a lot more money
Some clothes that are brand-new
These things I have are old-fashioned
Is that the best that You can do?

And as I fall asleep
I realize it's true
I am a spoiled thankless child
His mercy is the best that He can do

> For since the creation of the world His invisible attributes, His eternal power and divine nature, have been clearly seen, being understood through what has been made, so that they are without excuse. For even though they knew God, they did not honor Him as God or give thanks, but they became futile in their speculations, and their foolish heart was darkened. Professing to be wise, they became fools. (Rom 1:21–22)

Submission, Not Permission

You ask so very much of Me
You seek only My permission
You fail to recognize or see
I accept only full submission

I am not here to grant your wishes
Nor fill heartfelt desire
The miracle of the loaves and fishes
Was designed so you'd look higher

I know what's good and best for you
And I don't see it on your list
Submission to My will is what you must do
And that's the principle you missed

You seek permission, and I refuse
Because it's not within My will
You proceed and fail because you exclude
That I am Lord of all and still

I expect your full submission
Your body, your mind and soul
I only grant permission
For the things that make you whole

So when you come to pray to Me
Leave your list of selfish requests
A submissive heart is what I want to see
And to that I always answer yes

And whatsoever ye shall ask in my name, that will I do, that the Father may be glorified in the Son. (Jn 14:13)

Ye ask, and receive not, because ye ask amiss, that ye may consume it upon your lusts. (Jas 4:3 KJV)

Me or You

At the end of the day
Seeing things in rear view
I must ask myself
Did they see me,
Or did they see You?

I can be so very charming
I have jokes that are new
I am witty and so learned
Did they see me,
Or did they see You?

I wear what is fashionable
Things afforded by few
As they look at my wardrobe
Did they see me,
Or did they see You?

My opinions are highly valued
People quote me—they do
The flesh is fed; the spirit is empty
Looking at me
They couldn't see You

He must increase, but I must decrease.
(Jn 3:30)

He Always Celebrates You

While others notice your weakness
And the failures in what you would do
Your Father sees you as His own
And He always celebrates you

The world may see you as useless
Nothing good from their point of view
But your Father sees you as precious
And He always celebrates you

Even you keep an account of your losses
You accuse and cast aspersions on you
But your Father sees your perfection
And He always celebrates you

As you enter the world each day
Recognize that most have no clue
Few know your Father sees joy
And He always celebrates you

> Behold what manner of love the father hath
> bestowed upon us that we should be called sons
> of God: therefore the world knoweth us not
> because it knew him not. (1 Jn 3:1)

Amend It

Jesus, I did say yes to You
I'd like now to amend it
I'd like to reconsider
If not, can I rescind it?

You make such great and wild demands
You want me to be pure
But if I live the way You want
I'd be an oddball, that's for sure

I'd like for You to bend the curve
Lower the bar, I mean
Set a different standard for me, Lord
Like somewhere in between

The good people and the not so bad
Your holiness just won't do
I can look good compared to them
I have a reputation too

So let's negotiate, dear Lord
You said I could call You friend
I'll take one step; You do the same
We establish this new trend

We can compromise on everything
We can ignore that thing called sin
Then I paused to hear His answer
"Foolish man, you never will get in

"For I know Mine and they know Me
I know you just pretend
We never had an agreement
Hell's fire is your end"

> And why call ye me, Lord, Lord, and do not the things which I say? (Lk 6:46)
>
> And then I will declare to them, "I never knew you; depart from Me." (Mt 7:23)
>
> Then shall he say also unto them on the left hand, Depart from me, ye cursed, into everlasting fire, prepared for the devil and his angels. (Mt 25:41)
>
> And he will answer, "I tell you, I do not know where you are from. Depart from me, all you evildoers." (Lk 13:27)

Grudges

Life is too short to hold grudges
To cherish and remember each pain
And death is too close to be bitter
To rehearse offenses again and again

Let go of the past and the failures
Disappointments and promises broken
Deeds done and not done—yes, it hurt you
Those were harsh words that were spoken

But if you cling to the worst of your past
If these are the thoughts that you nourish
You can never enjoy the best of the present
And for sure your future never will flourish

Oh yes, more bad memories still do await you
Sharp insults and evil deeds are ahead
But let the wound heal—it will scar
If it didn't, it would fester instead

And to fester is to hold on to grudges
Constantly relive the offense as if new
And if you claim Christ is your Lord
"Let it go" is His commandment to you

> For if you forgive men their trespasses your
> Heavenly Father will also forgive you. But if you
> do not forgive men their trespasses neither will
> your Father forgive yours. (Mt 6:14–15)

As far as the east is from the west, so far hath he removed our transgressions from us. (Ps 103:12)

For I will be merciful to their unrighteousness, and their sins and their iniquities will I remember no more. (Heb 8:12)

Shake Hands with the Devil

An old preacher once told me
Not so long ago
If you shake hands with the devil
It is hard to let go

He will grant your desires
But just so you know
He's the master of deceit
The Bible says so

You will defeat your opponents
Your influence and power will grow
But it will be only on his terms
You see, he's the real foe

So once your hand is in his
He will have you in tow
And as the old preacher said
It is hard to let go

> When he speaketh a lie, he speaketh of his
> own: for he is a liar, and the father of it. (Jn 8:44)
> And no marvel; for Satan himself is trans-
> formed into an angel of light. (2 Cor 11:14)

The One Thing She Could Do

Your mama left you with me
I've no money to care for you
Take off your clothes; go to that man
It was the one thing she could do

She was twelve years old and frightened
He was old and smelly too
She had no defense to his advance
It was the one thing she could do

Her body changed; she wondered why
Something inside her grew
You dare not have that baby here
It was the one thing she could do

The doctor was not nice at all
Her office smelled of mildew
"Lie on this bed," she commanded
It was the one thing she could do

No place to sleep, no food to eat
Clothes worn and tattered too
Come here, sweet thing, and give me some
It was the one thing she could do

Body worn and good for nothing
Her choices were so few
Pleasure others with her body
It was the one thing she could do

Don't judge me was her thought
As she lay down on the church pew
It was warm and quiet; she fell asleep
It was the one thing she could do

She heard the voice of angels
She asked, "Lord, is that You"
He said, "Come home, My child. You're welcome"
It was the one thing she could do

Jesus went across to Mount Olives, but he was soon back in the Temple again. Swarms of people came to him. He sat down and taught them.

The religion scholars and Pharisees led in a woman who had been caught in an act of adultery. They stood her in plain sight of everyone and said, "Teacher, this woman was caught red-handed in the act of adultery. Moses, in the Law, gives orders to stone such persons. What do you say?" They were trying to trap him into saying something incriminating so they could bring charges against him.

Jesus bent down and wrote with his finger in the dirt. They kept at him, badgering him. He straightened up and said, "The sinless one among you, go first: Throw the stone." Bending down again, he wrote some more in the dirt.

Hearing that, they walked away, one after another, beginning with the oldest. The woman was left alone. Jesus stood up and spoke to her. "Woman, where are they? Does no one condemn you?" "No one, Master." "Neither do I," said Jesus. "Go on your way. From now on, don't sin." (Jn 8:1–11)

Default to Self

When there are choices to be made
Like two things on a shelf
Between comfort and correctness
I choose default to self

When I am sure no one is watching
Just me and no one else
I don't have to consider feelings
I prefer default to self

I want the things that I want
I'm no moral giant but an elf
Greed and ego overwhelm me
In sin I default to self

> Let this mind be in you which was also in
> Christ Jesus: who being in the form of God,
> thought it not robbery to be equal with God:
> but made himself of no reputation and took
> upon him the form of a servant and was made in
> the likeness of men. And being found in fashion
> as a man he humbled himself, and became obe-
> dient unto death, even the death of the cross.
> (Phil 2:4–8)

I Rebuild

I rebuild what is broken
I mend what's torn apart
My word once fitly spoken
Heals both soul and heart

Your bruised and broken feelings
Wounds and scars that make you cringe
Painful signs, distorted healing
Still makes each muscle twinge

Those bad memories so vivid
Things in your brain now seared
Makes your anger real and livid
Relive the things you feared

I am all you need to calm
I am Who soothes and brings release
I am the healing balm
I am the Prince of peace

> O LORD my God, I cried out to You, and you healed me. (Ps 30:2)
>
> But unto you that fear my name shall the Sun of righteousness arise with healing in his wings; and ye shall go forth, and grow up as calves of the stall. (Mal 4:2)
>
> And Jesus saith unto him, "I will come and heal him." (Mt 8:7)

He Listens

When everyone else has answers
When everyone else has positions
When everyone else has conclusions
My Savior holds me and listens

When everyone else has no doubts
When everyone else has decisions
When everyone else has their minds closed
My Savior hugs me and listens

When everyone else still remembers
When they conclude my guilt without condition
When everyone else walks away
My Savior stands with me and listens

He doesn't care if I am right or am wrong
He doesn't care if I've made pure contrition
What matters to Him is my salvation
So my Savior comforts and listens

If you are struggling with the pain of opinions
If others hold you in contempt and derision
If you are filled with self-doubt and regret
Come to Christ Jesus—He will listen

> This poor man cried, and the Lord heard
> him, and saved him out of all his troubles. O
> taste and see that the Lord is good: blessed is the
> man that trusteth in him. (Ps 34:6, 8)

Just Twenty-Six Hours

Lord, make my day twenty-six hours
That adds up to two hours more
Just think of the things I could do
If not limited to just twenty-four

Lord, You must understand
I am busy and need more time
Just 120 minutes extra
I could accomplish both Your will and mine

Two shifts of thirteen full hours
Bathroom and food breaks in between
Sleep and play are merely distractions
Not quite as important as they seem

If You could do so much in one day
Just think how much more I could do
I know it adds fourteen hours each week
Ignore the math; concentrate on just two

So as You consider my prayers
Remember this simple request
On second thought make it three hours
I can use the third one to rest

My times are in thy hand. (Ps 31:15)

Just Nod

The Holy Spirit gave me this word
I am sure it came from God
Never write when you can speak
Never speak when you can nod

If you must put pen to paper
Once the ink has left its stain
Consider the heart of who is reading
It is hard to erase the pain

If you must speak, do so softly
Draws attention to each word
Makes everyone listen very closely
They are clear about what they heard

Be aware that your opinions
Don't have the gravity of God
Hold your tongue; put the pen down
Never speak when you can nod

> Wherefore, my beloved brethren, let every man be swift to hear, slow to speak, slow to wrath. (Jas 1:19)

Next Shiny Thing

I want to confess You are Lord
I want to confess You as King
But just when I am ready to speak
I discuss the next shiny thing

You are worthy of all honor and glory
More worthy than any gift I can bring
Your majesty and splendor obscured
As I admire the next shiny thing

I want to adore You and worship
With words that I speak and I sing
But just as I open my mouth
I speak only of the next shiny thing

Creator God, sweet Savior, Sustainer
Holy Ghost sending angels on wings
Please protect me from even myself
So I don't chase the next shiny thing

> For the love of money is the root of all evil:
> which while some coveted after, they have erred
> from the faith, and pierced themselves through
> with many sorrows. (1 Tm 6:10)
>
> That they do good, that they be rich in
> good works, ready to distribute, willing to com-
> municate. (1 Tm 6:18)
>
> Labour not to be rich: cease from thine own
> wisdom. (Prv 23:4)
>
> He also that received seed among the thorns
> is he that heareth the word; and the care of this
> world, and the deceitfulness of riches, choke the
> word, and he becometh unfruitful. (Mt 13:22)

Those

It only makes a difference
I would suppose
When we are they
And us are those

When they are killed
Way over there
No blood on me
Why should I care?

We are safe and protected
Away from the mob
We are clean and untouched
While they rape, steal, and rob

But if we are they
If one of us offends
We disclaim our own
Well, he never fit in

He's not one of us
He is one of those
Don't let him return
Keep that door closed

If our liberty is suppressed
If our rights are offended
Our outrage would rise
We would rise to defend it

But when they cry out foul
With loud moans and great tears
We shout out, "Be quiet!"
As we cover our ears

Listen, you over there
As everyone knows
You are not one of us
You are just one of those

> For there is no respect of persons with God.
> (Rom 2:11)

Tit for Tat

She said this
I said that
And so we keep trading
Tit for tat

I asked why
She said 'cause
And we never settle
On what is or was

I voted no
She wrote yes
And now we revel
In what is a mess

No need to agree
Just argue no more
Opinions and facts
Not worth fighting for

Learn to let go
Let the other one win
To be always on top
Is also called sin

> Do nothing out of selfish ambition or vain conceit but in humility consider others better than yourselves. Each of you should look not only to your own interests but also the interests of others. (Phil 2:3–4)

My Short List

I have my very own short list
Of people I ignore
Those who have offended me
I can now even the score

I pretend I just don't see them
As if they didn't exist
They wronged and they hurt me
That's why they are on my list

When on the street I see them
I cross to the other side
If they try to come and greet me
I increase my speed and stride

I compared my list to God's
He was not picky as expected
He had a lower standard
He listed none rejected

He informed me of His choices
Of His lowering the bar
Said that if He judged as I did
Even I wouldn't make it far

He said, "I have no list of left-outs
Those I refuse to recognize
All are equally sinful and unworthy
But I do not one despise

"I offer them all salvation
I grant them heaven's bliss
And for Me to welcome you
You must take them off your list

"Your list of unforgiven
Your list of 'rot in hell'
Your list of 'that's the last straw'
If you can't, then I will tell

"That you have no name in heaven
For you eternity does not exist
If you call yourself My child
You have no hate on your list"

> 2 Peter 3:8–9 Beloved, do not let this one thing escape your notice: With the Lord a day is like a thousand years, and a thousand years are like a day. The Lord is not slow to fulfill His promise as some understand slowness, but is patient with you not wanting anyone to perish, but everyone to come to repentance.

A Pretty Bauble

A pretty bauble
A shiny bead
Just out of reach
Not what I need

A thing to fancy
A thing to want
To tickle, enamor
To tease, to taunt

This constant hunger
This unfulfilled lust
This displaced affection
Traps this frame of dust

Can I loosen this grip?
Can I be free from its lure?
Yes, there is a way out
There is a real cure

> I find then a law, that, when I would do good, evil is present with me. For I delight in the law of God after the inward man: But I see another law in my members, warring against the law of my mind, and bringing me into captivity to the law of sin which is in my members. *O wretched man that I am! who shall deliver me from the body of this death?* I thank God through Jesus Christ our Lord. So then with the mind I myself serve the law of God; but with the flesh the law of sin. (Rom 7:21–25, emphasis added)

What's Next

I am still learning to surrender
I am still learning to let go
I am still learning to be still
Because this one thing I know

I can trust the future to Him
Nothing comes as a surprise
He knows what page is turning
He has seen the next sunrise

Nothing catches Him off balance
Nothing catches Him unprepared
Nothing makes Him ask "What happened?"
For He alone declared

I am alpha and omega
I hold all in balance and in check
Don't try to plan your life without Me
I alone can say "what's next"

> Go to now, ye that say, Today or tomorrow we will go into such a city, and continue there a year, and buy and sell, and get gain: Whereas ye know not what shall be on the morrow.
>
> For what is your life? It is even a vapour, that appeareth for a little time, and then vanisheth away. For that ye ought to say, If the Lord will, we shall live, and do this, or that. But now ye rejoice in your boastings: all such rejoicing is evil. Therefore to him that knoweth to do good, and doeth it not, to him it is sin. (Jas 4:13–17)

I Will Never Forgive You

I never have to forgive you
I never have to show sorrow
So if that is what you're expecting
You can wait a many tomorrow

For I felt wounded when you upset me
I felt cheated, alone, and left out
Now I just want to protect me
That I will do without doubt

It is easier for me to hold on to
The pain from the problems you caused
For if I really had to forgive you
I would have to give vengeance a pause

When I really stop to consider
The arrogance of my strong stance
I bow down; I must surrender
I must give Christ's love a chance

For if I truly want His peace
And if I want His best in my life
There is only one way this can happen
I must cease from all things that cause strife

> Vengeance is mine; I will repay, saith the
> Lord. Be not overcome of evil, but overcome evil
> with good. (Rom 12:19, 21)

Help Someone Today

I talked to my Father this morning
Before I got out of bed to stand
He told me to kneel down before Him
Then He gave me this simple command

He said, "My dear son, please remember
That each breath that comes in and out of your lungs
Gives you strength to help others less fortunate
Whose days are ending just as yours has begun

"Do all that you can, dear child, to help others
Make it a point to find purpose and fill needs
It is so easy to fall into the traps the world offers
To fill your own hunger and greed

"Before you return to your bed this evening
Find someone to cheer with a word or a smile
Make a point, seek them out, and be aware
It is this that will make your day truly worthwhile

"As you stand up to begin this new day
I will be with you to make sure you succeed
I will comfort, protect, and provide you
When you lie down, you'll have the sleep that you need

"Go in My strength and change the world for someone today

> For I was an hungred, and ye gave me
> meat: I was thirsty, and ye gave me drink: I was
> a stranger, and ye took me in: Naked, and ye
> clothed me: I was sick, and ye visited me: I was
> in prison, and ye came unto me. (Mt 25:35–36)

Imagine This
Imagine That

A love so good
A love so true
A love aimed at only you

A love that comforts
A love that restores
A love that's freely, freely yours

Imagine this
Imagine that
My true love is where it's at

I give to you what no one else can give
The gift of Myself
A real chance to live

Free from guilt
Free from pain
Coming to Me is truly gain

Imagine this
Imagine that
My true love is where it's at

> Come unto me, all ye that labor and are
> heavy laden, and I will give you rest. (Mt 11:28)

Live in Your Past

I choose to live in your past
You choose to move on to tomorrow
For you the pain does not last
It is I who still bear sorrow

You have long buried your mistakes
I move backward, digging them up again
How long to forgive will it take?
I keep rehearsing your failure and sin

Will I ever grow weary of trying to find
The things that you have buried in the ground?
Why does it still possess my mind?
Why do I want your past weakness found?

It is a fault I refuse to release
It is a habit I refuse to let go
I am afraid you have found such great peace
A peace that I'll never know

I will continue to follow and haunt
Each time you fall, I'll be there
I will make fun, tease, and taunt
I'll make sure you have burdens to bear

If God forgives you, I still don't
If He forgets, I will remind
It's not that I can't—I just won't
And this illness is what kills and binds

> And whenever ye may stand praying, forgive, if ye have anything against any one, that your Father also who is in the heavens may forgive you your trespasses. (Mk 11:25)

Stand Naked, My Child

I stood there naked before you
You knew I had nothing to hide
My skin ripped, bloodied, torn through
My heart bursting, crying inside

The beatings though mean and so vicious
Were not nearly as painful or cruel
As the eyes full of hate, so malicious
On the faces of Satan's tools

Yes, he used you to strip and bring shame
To humiliate and lead Me to death
I called out My dear Father's name
As I took My last living breath

If you will stand naked before Me
I will place on you clothing of peace
I will impart My own glory to you
You must first your own vesture release

All your shame and pain is what I bore
The self-loathing, self-doubt, and deep fear
These garments only defile more
Take them off at the cross; leave them there

Deny self—it's a garment unworthy
Of a child of My Father, the King
Your self-pride is a covering that's dirty
Take it off; wear My robe and My ring

Stand naked, My child; let Me clothe you

I will greatly rejoice in the LORD, my soul shall be joyful in my God; for he hath clothed me with the garments of salvation, he hath covered me with the robe of righteousness, as a bridegroom decketh himself with ornaments, and as a bride adorneth herself with her jewels. (Is 61:10)

Another Chance

Today God gave me another chance
Although I misused His name and His grace
He continued to extend His hand of mercy
He showed me His kind, loving face

He did not recall to me my evil past
Although I did recall and know
He told me His anger would not long last
He had long since let it go

So if God gives me another chance
Even when I continue to fail and fall
I must extend the same mercy to you
And no longer your past recall

I vow to never speak of the wrong
Of which I perceived and accused you
For in remembering and rehearsing the past pain and hurt
I cut short God's own mercy that's new

I will show mercy as He has done
I will give pardon as God did to me
For just as He through mercy has my heart won
My mercy and grace must be free

To forgive you is freeing; I am no longer in jail
I no longer have to be bitter and unkind
But to hold to your past and make you still pay
Does not damage your heart, just mine

Then his lord, after that he had called him,
said unto him, O thou wicked servant, I forgave

thee all that debt, because thou desiredst me: Shouldest not thou also have had compassion on thy fellow servant, even as I had pity on thee? And his lord was wroth, and delivered him to the tormentors, till he should pay all that was due unto him. (Mt 18:32–34)

Would I

If I had the chance to do it over
Would I take that chance to do it better?
Would I treat you a little kinder?
Would I not have sent that letter?

Would I seek time to reconcile?
Would I turn to give embrace?
Would I give you a bright smile
Or turn a less friendly face?

When you have loss, would I too weep?
When you have joy, would I rejoice?
When you are in pain, would I lose sleep?
When you're lost for words, would I lend my voice?

If I had the chance to do it over
Would I take that chance to do it right?
Would I continue to sin in dark cover?
Or would I live in God's clean light?

I don't have the chance to do it over
But I do have time to make it good
And if God gives me another day
I have determined that I would

> Redeeming the time because the days are
> evil. (Eph 5:16)
> Walk in wisdom toward them that are with-
> out redeeming the time. (Col 4:5)

I Withheld My Love

I withheld my love from you
I thought you did not deserve it
Although you needed a smile
I chose instead to reserve it

I freely gave my affection
To others, to people outside
Your need for approval meant nothing
When compared to my own selfish pride

No matter that it was your need
Big or small though it might be
I chose to completely ignore it
And instead I focused on me

The touch you so often requested
The hugs you continued to crave
The encouraging words you desired
Instead of you, for others I saved

Oh, one day I will release these
I will let you feel my soft touch
But don't ask me to do it right now
It is really expecting too much

There is something that is truly disturbing
About my list of these preconditions
Though you want to draw near, I refuse it
I won't give you such permission

I know it does not reflect Jesus
He never refuses embrace
So if I really want to accept His love
I must also extend you His grace

> Withhold not good from them to whom it
> is due, when it is in the power of thine hand to
> do it. (Prv 3:27)

A Better World

Is the world a little brighter?
Is the world a better place?
Is any burden a little lighter
Because I have left a trace?

Have I given joy to any?
Have I helped someone to smile?
Have I eased the load of many?
Have I gone the extra mile?

Or is my life focused only
On the things that please my flesh?
Do I comfort the wounded, the lonely
Or do I open wounds afresh?

Do I stand and give critique
When asked for counsel and advice?
When plain answers are what they seek
Do I reflect the mind of Christ?

Lord, I pray that You bring change
May that change begin with me
Increase my influence and my range
As my life is hid in Thee

>Is not this the fast that I have chosen: to loose the bonds of wickedness, to undo the bands of the yoke, and to let the oppressed go free, and that ye break every yoke? Is it not to deal thy bread to the hungry, and that thou bring the poor that are cast out to thy house? when thou seest the naked, that thou cover him; and that thou hide not thyself from thine own flesh. (Is 58:6–7)

Make the Devil Smile

I know how to please the devil
I know how to make him smile
I pretend that I forgive you
While holding grudges all the while

I go to church on Sunday
And on occasion read my Bible too
But from every weekday from that Monday
I remember the wrong things that you do

I keep a close account
Of the things that make you fall and fail
When you make mistakes and falter
I make sure I do others tell

When you smite me on my one cheek
I make sure to smite you back
Though I know I should forgive you
That would require a different tack

I keep my secret sins
Of anger, lust, and greed
I ignore the poor and lonely
I focus on my own needs

I ignore you when I see you
I refuse to pray your peace
When you fall, it gives me pleasure
That your miseries increase

I keep my faith a secret
Don't let others know the Christ I love
People I don't like might get saved
I don't want to see them up above

I am good at pleasing Satan
I am on his side without relent
I know I don't please Jesus
Pray with me that I will repent

> He that is not with me is against me; and
> he that gathereth not with me scattereth abroad.
> (Mt 12:30)

Afraid to Abide

I am afraid to open my Bible
I am afraid of what it might say
It might even start a revival
I will have to do things God's way

I am afraid to get close to Jesus
I am afraid to walk by His side
He threatened to make me more like Him
If I would let Him near to abide

So I stay as far away as I can
Keep the music and TV on loud and clear
I drown out His voice and His calling
Influenced only by what I see and I hear

This fear of course does not help me
It keeps me from being the best that I can
One day I must claim the Savior
I'll regret deeply the days that I ran

> If ye abide in me, and my words abide in
> you, ye shall ask what ye will, and it shall be done
> unto you. (Jn 15:7)

I Have a Secret

There is a secret I refuse to tell
On how you can keep your soul from hell
I learned it from others who knew it too
But I am too embarrassed to share it with you

I know it sounds strange and maybe quite cruel
But if I shared this with you, I would feel like a fool
After all do I have a right to my faith impose
Upon others like you who believe different, I suppose?

So I just keep quiet and let you believe as you want
I won't discuss my beliefs—it is a tease and a taunt
I believe I'll get heaven, but I'll leave you to your way
If you did that to me, I'd have something to say

Why should I leave others in a way that is damned
When I know how to help them take the truly right stand?
I suppose those are questions that are worth asking twice
I would answer to you; I was trying to be nice.

I did not want to be pushy and offend
So I let you believe I was truly your friend
When in fact if I loved you and knew that heaven was real
I would reconsider the way that I felt

I would share with you what others shared with me
I would make it my duty to help you truly see
That Christ is the way, the truth, and the light
To share Jesus with you is all that is right

> Go ye therefore, and teach all nations…the
> Son, and of the Holy Ghost. (Mt 28:19)

I Don't Want Holiness

I don't want holiness
If I can't have You
If You aren't my joy
Keep that away too

I don't want food
Nor water for my thirst
If Christ isn't with me
You see, I need Christ first

I don't want health
Family nor close friend
I need Christ most
My beginning and end

You can keep heaven
In deep hell I'd be
If Christ isn't there
Eternal life is endless misery

I would rather have death,
Jesus, than life without You
For eternity at best
Is only torment anew

> Whom have I in heaven but thee? and there
> is none upon earth that I desire beside thee. (Ps
> 73:25)

Easy to Love

It's easy to love those who love you
The devils and demons fill that role
But to love those whom you feel don't deserve it
Is the real call on each Christian's soul

For true love is oft unrewarded
At least not right now nor right here
True love finds its greatest triumph
In drawing the most difficult enemy near

If we cannot love God through each other
Then we cannot love Him really at all
For our Father in heaven is most pleased
When we fulfill this singular call

For He loved me when I was unworthy
When I deserved hell, He gave me more grace
When I cursed and abused His name
When I lived life in unashamed disgrace

So embrace those whom you feel most unworthy
Of your kindness or your loving touch
You must love those who aren't like you
Of this love the kingdom of heaven is such

> But I say unto you, Love your enemies,
> bless them that curse you, do good to them that
> hate you, and pray for them which despitefully
> use you, and persecute you;
> For if ye love them which love you, what
> reward have ye? do not even the publicans the
> same? Be ye therefore perfect, even as your Father
> which is in heaven is perfect. (Mt 5:44, 46, 48)

How Do I Know

How do I know you love Jesus?
Because I know you love me
For to love one and not the other
Is impossible as you can see

For to love Christ you must first enter
A relationship with those here at hand
If God is at your life's true center
Then you will follow this simple command

As you love those here down below
And this covenant is truly for real
You do so not just for show
Not for fashion but true godly zeal

That is how I know you love Jesus
Because it is clearly shown in your deeds
And as you love me it assures
The Father will supply all your needs

> If a man say, I love God, and hateth his
> brother, he is a liar: for he that loveth not his
> brother whom he hath seen, how can he love God
> whom he hath not seen? And this commandment
> have we from him, That he who loveth God love
> his brother also. (1 Jn 4:20–21)

Loved, Not Led

I want to be loved by You but not led
Provide the food in Your hand so I'm fed
Let me bear Your good name
Let me bathe in Your fame
Besides that I'll choose my own ways instead

For I know that You lead in a narrow path
In the middle grace and on either side wrath
If I abide in Your will
It requires that I be still
And let the words that You say be the last

Such is my sin of presumption
To know what is best for my life by assumption
As I ignore the wisdom of ages
If I resent the Sage of all sages
I will miss my true purpose and function

> But he that sinneth against me wrongeth his own soul: all they that hate me love death. (Prv 8:36)
> There is a way which seemeth right unto a man, but the end thereof are the ways of death. (Prv 14:12)

I Wish You Away

I wish You'd go away
Let me do things as I want
But You hang around my door
As if to tease and taunt

You tell me of Your love
Your care and sacrifice
I don't really want to hear it
Just let me live my life

You think that Your entreaties
Will make me change my mind
You only strengthen my resolve
To leave Your will behind

I would rather continue without You
Though I must admit You give
Each precious breath I take
The heart that lets me live

You provide me health and wholeness
You provide me food and home
Even when I ignore You
You don't leave me alone

So I must admit I need You
Yes, I need You in my life
Don't go; instead, come closer
Keep me from sin and strife

I open the door to receive You
I will receive Your outstretched arms
Your comfort, hugs, and kisses
Your protection from all harms

Welcome, Lord Jesus
Please come in

> Behold, I stand at the door, and knock: if
> any man hear my voice, and open the door, I will
> come in to him, and will sup with him, and he
> with me. (Rv 3:20)

Closer to You

All the good that I had hoped for
All the best that I can do
Can mean nothing of real value
Unless it brings me close to You

For You alone can keep me
You alone protect
You alone are worthy
Holy, pure, good, perfect

I can have all the world can offer
Acquire gold, amass great wealth
Buy You alone give life
You alone give health

All the good that I find within me
Is but dross and filthy pride
Until I allow Your will, Your way
Let You come and live inside

Help me, Father, to seek the good
That only comes from Your kind hand
I will find true peace and comfort
I kneel first; then with You I stand

> And he said unto him, Why callest thou me
> good? there is none good but one, that is, God:
> but if thou wilt enter into life, keep the com-
> mandments. (Mt 19:17)

I Am Worthy

I am worthy of your honor
I am worthy of your praise
I am He Who gives you life
I am He Who gives you days

You can ignore Me and forget
You can refuse to call My name
But you will very soon regret
And your pride will turn to shame

Call on Me for I am waiting
Praise Me for My healing power
Thank Me for My provision
Think on Me every minute, every hour

For indeed I alone Am worthy
Yes, indeed I alone provide
If you want true peace and wisdom
You will let Me live inside

> I will praise thee, O Lord, with my whole
> heart; I will shew forth all thy marvelous works.
> (Ps 9:1)

A Fresh Fight

Every day I fight afresh
The desire to satisfy my flesh
The cravings of my sinful mind
Are common to all mankind

My envy, lust, and prideful heart
These things keep me far apart
From what God intended I should be
The man He wants to make of me

However, I leave my mind to go
To places where no light can show
The deepest, darkest sinful deeds
I know as desires, I call them needs

The jealous and unforgiving themes
The lies and gossip and other schemes
To make me look much better than
The other whom I call ordinary man

But for God's mercy I would lose this fight
And continue in this hell-bound plight
I am kept by mercy and saved by grace
Without my Savior, I would lose this race

> This I say then, Walk in the Spirit, and ye
> shall not fulfil the lust of the flesh. (Gal 5:16)

I Hated the Sound

I hated the sound of Your name
It reminded me of my filth and my shame
So I chose to ignore
When You knocked on my door
And instead waited 'till someone else came

He did not even knock to come in
He had the keys to all types of sin
He offered each type
With great pomp and such hype
And after all I just wanted to fit in

So I shook hands with this visitor of mine
He was polite; he was generous and kind
He gave me all that I asked
He requested only on tasks
That he allowed that my heart he could bind

After years of serving this bad master
I came to realize what he was after
It was my soul he did crave
And so freely I gave
Without realizing I had already been captured

But You came to my door and knocked again
You bid me to please let You in
I was praying with my knees on the floor
Got up and opened the door
I now call You Lord, Savior, Friend

> Behold, I stand at the door, and knock: if
> any man hear my voice, and open the door, I will
> come in to him, and will sup with him, and he
> with me. (Rv 3:20)

I Know How to Want!

I know how to want
But not how to need
My culture it taunts
With satisfied greed

My clothing, the latest
My colognes smell just right
My car is the greatest
I have all that delights

The word *need* doesn't fit
In my vocabulary or thoughts
It's that unwholesome bit
Of the dos and the oughts

I am fully content
With what I am told to desire
If I can't borrow or rent
I'll just pray to acquire

To know want is so simple
But I can't discern what to need
But my body, my temple
Is what God wants to feed

But godliness with contentment is great gain. For we brought nothing into this world, and it is certain we can carry nothing out And having food and raiment let us be therewith content.

But they that will be rich fall into temptation and a snare, and into many foolish and hurtful lusts, which drown men in destruction and perdition. For the love of money is the root of all evil: which while some coveted after, they have erred from the faith, and pierced themselves through with many sorrows. (1 Tm 6:6–10)

A Little Pruning

I told the Lord I'm worthy
Maybe a little of fine-tuning
He cut me very sharply
Said, "You really need some pruning"

I told the Lord I'm perfect
Maybe a bit of slight adjusting
He whipped out some big scissors
Said, "You really need some cutting"

I told the Lord I've made it
No correction needed here
He looked within his toolshed
And picked out the sharpest shears

I told Him, "Lord, You're picky
What fruit do you think I lack?"
He then pulled out a hatchet
And gave one branch a whack

He then spoke to me in terms
That any vine could understand
"Oh yes, you do produce well
But not yet the best you can

"The cuts I make are needed
For you continue to do your best
And since you are in My garden
I say who's passed the test"

> Every branch in me that beareth not fruit he
> taketh away: and every branch that bears fruit he
> purchased it, that it may bring forth more fruit.
> (Jn 15:2)

I Don't Remember That

I held my head in shame
First, I removed my hat
I failed You, Heavenly Father
He said, "I don't remember that"

But I know I disappoint You
My arrogant pride is fact
My Father smiled and said,
"I don't remember that"

I do the wrong I shouldn't
I revenge with tit for tat
My Father shook His head
"I don't remember that

"My child, when you confess your sin
I know if it's just an act
I see you through your Savior's blood
That's why I don't remember that"

> He will again turn he will have compassion upon us; he will subdue our iniquities and doubt will cast all their sins into the depths of the sea. (Mi 7:19)
>
> For as the heaven is high above the earth, so great is his mercy toward them that fear him. As far as the east is from the west, so far has he removed our transgressions from us. Like as a father pitieth his children, so the Lord pitieth them that fear him. For he knoweth our frame; he remembereth that we are dust. (Ps 103:11)

You Really Won't Need Me

I complain about my job
Just a low-pay employee
God said, "If it fulfills you
You really won't need Me"

I complain about my mate
My spouse is not what she should be
God said, "If she satisfies you
You really won't need Me"

I complain about my children
I am always right—they don't agree
God said, "If they mirror you
You really won't need Me"

I have made so many idols
On a pedestal for me to see
God said, "If I don't destroy them
You really won't need Me"

> Thou shalt have no other gods before me. (Ex 20:3)
>
> If any man come to me, and hate not his father, and mother, and wife, and children, and brethren, and sisters, yea, and his own life also, he cannot be my disciple. (Lk 14:26)

Dirty Sheep

The pastor prayed this prayer
"My Father, please do hear
Just give me clean sheep, Lord
Now let me make this clear

"Those with coats that shine
Not those matted with manure
I want this church of mine
To be spiritually mature

"Send me sheep that are well heeled
You know, financially, fat as pigs
So when I have appealed
They don't have far to dig

"They won't ask me for much
A decent sermon now and then
An occasional 'slain in the spirit touch'
No Bible standards to defend

"But those sheep smell and make noise
They are offensive to nose and ears
They take away the sweet joys
They are not equal to my peers

"In fact if it's no bother
Send other churches those unclean lambs
Just send me the goats, dear Father
I feel at ease with sparkling rams"

And with that prayer complete
He knew God indeed had heard
A goat instantly did bleat
God was true to His word

The church grew strong and vibrant
Every member with new cars and clothes
Not a stinky sheep among them
And not a single redeemed soul

> Beware of false prophets, which come to you in sheep's clothing, but inwardly they are ravening wolves. (Mt 7:15)
>
> And he shall set the sheep on his right hand, but the goats on the left. (Mt 25:33)

Give Me Power and Wealth

Lord, I want much more power
To do things truly great
Forgiving and loving to start with
Learning to be patient, to wait

Lord, I want to be wealthy
In good deeds and tender mercies
Closets and jewel boxes full
Lord, give me plenty of these

Make people to notice the difference
From the gifts in my life you bestow
Let them marvel with awe and wonder
That through me Your grace will show

> Neither do men light a candle and put it
> under a bushel, but on a candlestick; and it giveth
> light unto all that are in the house. Let your light
> so shine before men, that they may see your good
> works and glorify your father which is in heaven.
> (Mt 5:15–16)

Please, God, No Miracle

I don't want revelation
Just makes me work more
I prefer the situation
Stay as it was before

Miracles sound enticing
Special healings and such
Like sweet cake with the icing
Keep me from that spirit touch

If the spirit so desires
That I truly help the poor
Let Him first let me retire
Then I'll give a whole lot more

I am pleased that I acquire
Much more than I really need
All the things that I desire
All the stuff that fills my greed

Please, God, don't infuse me
With some miraculous insight
I would rather You excuse me
I don't want to do what's right

> You ask, and receive not, because ye ask amiss, that ye may consume it upon your lusts. (Jas 4:3)
>
> And whatsoever you shall ask in my name, that will I do, that the Father may be glorified in the Son. (Jn 14:13)

Bits and Pieces

I delivered your baby in pieces
Bits of flesh, a hand and then a foot
I tore it from your safe body
Threw to the trash with the soot

The heart had already stopped beating
I injected it with an adult overdose
So by the time I delivered those pieces
Was it alive? No, not even close

But the remnants put up a struggle
I scraped the remains from your womb
What God intended as nurture
I instead made it a tomb

I have no idea where those parts are
Those bits of flesh now have no breath
I delivered just bits and pieces
And I was paid for causing its death

> I will praise thee; for I am fearfully and
> wonderfully made: marvelous are thy works; and
> that my soul knows right well.
>
> My substance was not hid from thee, when
> I was made in secret, and curiously wrought in
> the lowest parts of the earth.
>
> Thine eyes did see my substance, yet being
> unperfect; and in thy book all my members
> were written, which in continuance were fash-
> ioned, when as yet there was none of them. (Ps
> 139:14–16)

Favor and Fault

I note his every fault
As I justify my favor
The evil he deserves
I'm glad he's not my neighbor

He is dirty, and he smells
He is ragged and quite rude
He is undisciplined, unclean
Has a nasty attitude

No wonder he's a failure
I earn the good that comes my way
He is obviously at fault
God favors me, I say

Because I do what's good
Avoid the evil that I see
I know God looks from heaven
Ignores him and favors me

But to think so is just sinful
For Jesus teaches this:
We live by grace unmerited
This simple truth I miss

Wanting to justify my favor
And remind him he has fallen
I forget I live by grace
And I don't fulfill my calling

To seek redemption and restoring
Dearest Father, I truly plead
Father, forgive his faults and failures
Show him favor; fulfill his need

The Pharisee stood and prayed thus with himself, God, I thank thee, that I am not as other men are, extortioners, unjust, adulterers, or even as this publican. I fast twice in the week, I give tithes of all that I possess. And the publican, standing afar off, would not lift up so much as his eyes unto heaven, but smote upon his breast, saying, God be merciful to me a sinner. I tell you, this man went down to his house justified rather than the other: for everyone that exalteth himself shall be abased; and he that humbleth himself shall be exalted. (Lk 11:14–18)

God Sees Differently

It is my observation
I am quite astute at this
I can judge and, yes, condemn
And rarely do I miss

I know how to discern
Between what's good and truly bad
And so when I am angry
I know that God is mad

I observe the deeds of men
Sins committed by the hand
I have a simple checklist
I keep score on how they stand

But God uses a different measure
He sees not whom they've come to be
He sees how He can make them
That is how He measured me

When I damn those I deem a failure
When I set myself apart
God reminds me He sees different
God measures from the heart

> But the Lord said unto Samuel, Look not on his countenance, or on the height of his stature; because I have refused him: for the Lord seeth not as man seeth; for man looketh on the outward appearance, but the Lord looketh on the heart. (1 Sm 16:7)

Give Me Your Body

Give Me your body
Just as I gave you Mine
A seductive request
From the Savior divine

I have seen you naked before
I saw your parents conceive
About you not a thing I ignore
This one truth please believe

I'll shield you from fire
I'll keep you by grace
From filth, muck, and mire
You will have no disgrace

Give Me your thoughts
Release to Me your whole mind
The temptations you fought
The sins that still bind

I'll give you good rest
I'll cleanse and make pure
When you are put to a test
Your success will be sure

Give Me your love
Your hopes and your dreams
Think on things up above
Not on things as they seem

Make Me your desire
Make Me your heart's treasure
Of My love you won't tire
It's not transient pleasure

I'll add delight to your smile
I'll make your soul feel complete
Former lovers and friends
Cannot really compete

I know where to touch you
Where it hurts, how to soothe
I created your body
I know where you're bruised

If true love is your hunger
If it's true peace you seek
Look no further, no longer
I am the Lover Who is meek

> I beseech you therefore brethren, by the mercies of God, that you present your bodies a living sacrifice, holy, acceptable unto God, which is your reasonable service. (Rom 12:1)

Loving You

Loving you is easy
Love is Who and what I am
It is My nature, My very person
All other love's a scam

Behind the curtain and the veil
I know your weakness and your past
I have seen you when you failed
My love alone will last and last

Though your father and your mother
May not hear, know, or see your heart
I love you like no other
Others die, and they depart

I love you; yes, I love you
You are really Mine and Mine alone
I made you; I sustain you
I did for your sin atone

Rest assured and rest in peace
Know that all you need is Who I am
Remember—yes, remember—that I love you

All other love's a scam

       He that loveth not knoweth not God; for
God is love. (1 Jn 4:8)

I Looked At Your Sin

I looked closer at your sin
And mine looked even worse
I had assumed you as unworthy
When it was I who deserved the curse

The deeper I descended
Into the well of your dark past
The greater God's light showed
His mercy did outlast

So as I looked
Beneath the lashes
To see the splinter in your eye
The reflection in your pupil

Gave me cause to wonder why
Why is my God so merciful?
Why is God so kind?
I do and think such evil

And He doesn't seem to mind
For if God can overlook
My failings, faults, and selfishness
He can bring deliverance

He can handle anybody's mess!

> Don't pick on people, jump on their failures, criticize their faults—unless, of course, you want the same treatment. Don't condemn those who are down; that hardness can boomerang. Be easy on people; you'll find life a lot easier.

Give away your life; you'll find life given back, but not merely given back—given back with bonus and blessing. Giving, not getting, is the way. Generosity begets generosity. (Lk 6:37–38 MSG)

Either how canst thou say to thy brother, Brother, let me pull out the mote that is in thine eye, when thou thyself beholdest not the beam that is in thine own eye?

Thou hypocrite, cast out first the beam out of thine own eye, and then shalt thou see clearly to pull out the mote that is in thy brother's eye. (Lk 6:42 KJV)

When saw we thee a stranger, and took thee in? or naked, and clothed thee? Or when saw we thee sick, or in prison, and came unto thee?

And the King shall answer and say unto them, Verily I say unto you, Inasmuch as ye have done it unto one of the least of these my brethren, ye have done it unto me. (Mt 25:38–40)

Never Dine with the Atheist

The atheist knows there is no god
Mankind alone is to blame
For if there was a true deity
He should hang his head in shame

For all the suffering he lets unfold
And all the misery allowed
The atheist can clearly see
No mystery beyond the cloud

All faiths are mere creations
Of mankind trying to find
Reason and revelation
Ways to ease his troubled mind

All faiths are truly equal
Feed your neighbor; share your bread
You can also worship your god
By cutting off your neighbor's head

Because if evil is defined
By circumstance and culture
I can worship the god I want to
Slaying your children on my altar

But if there is a true goodness
And if there truly is bad
There must be ultimate perfection
A true treasure to be had

It can't be relatively speaking
It can't be both hot and cold
Both positrons and neutrons
Cannot the same position hold

My dear lost atheist, my friend
I may be wrong, and you are right
When you invite me to your table
I pray you will have bread tonight

He Calls You His

Some call you by title
Dr., Mr., or Ms.
But your Father has one name
He calls you His

Some know you by report
By your stuff you are known
Your Father has just one name
He calls you His own

Some see your failures
What you are and you ain't
Your shortcomings God sees
And He calls you saint

Don't bother with regret
Trying to impress all the others
Christ sees you as friend
He calls you sister and brother

> Ye are my friends if you do whatsoever I command you. Henceforth I call you not servants; for the servant know if not his Lord doeth: what I have called you friends; for all things that I have heard of my Father I have made known unto you. (Jn 15:14–15)

Always Here

When you feel lost, confused
The path forward is not clear
I Am the Way walks with you
I Am is always here

In the midst of all the debates
When you can't know who's sincere
I Am the Word speaks to you
I Am is always here

When you feel betrayed and lonely
And overwhelmed with fear
I Am Faithful stands with you
I Am is always here

In the time of death and sorrow
You lose those who are most dear
I Am the Comforter is right beside you
I Am is always here

As the end of life approaches
When you see that time is near
I Am Eternal welcomes you
I Am is always here

> Jesus saith unto him, I am the way, the truth, and the life: no man cometh unto the Father, but by me. (Jn 14:6)
>
> Be strong and of a good courage, fear not, nor be afraid of them: for the Lord thy God, he it is that doth go with thee; he will not fail thee, nor forsake thee. (Dt 31:6)

Does Jesus Do Voice Mail?

It may sound just a bit absurd
And maybe to blaspheme
Inconsistent with God's holy Word
But consistent with a theme

How could the Holy Trinity
Be bothered with every call?
Do They divide the work in three?
Are They listening to us all?

Do calls ever get lost or dropped?
Can the inbox overfill?
Does Their Internet connection ever stop
If They forget to pay the bill?

Does the Creator God really care
That I am self-centered and self-righteous?
Does He snicker at a selfish prayer
Then ignore it just to spite us?

I know I speak rhetorically
Comedic at its best
Of course God listens to every plea
So let's put this to rest

None goes unnoticed nor ignored
By this Holy Trinity
Of course You don't do voice mail, Lord
The one not listening is me

Hear this, you foolish and senseless people, who have eyes but do not see, who have ears but do not hear. (Jer 5:21)

Having eyes, see ye not? And having ears, hear ye not? (Mk 8:18)

Enjoy the Ride

Father, are we there yet?
My anxiety I could not hide
You said we'd be there soon
He said, Enjoy the ride

Could we be lost? I asked
Doesn't that road divide?
Didn't we pass that sign before?
He said, Enjoy the ride

I tried another tactic now
Thinking He'd notice if I cried
I'm hungry, and I am so bored
He said, Enjoy the ride

You already have arrived, my son
Your joy can't be denied
I am your destination
He said, Enjoy the ride

I am the way, the truth, the life
Put your maps and plans aside
When you have Me, no need to travel
Sit back and enjoy the ride

> Jesus saith unto him, I am the way, the truth,
> and the life: no man cometh unto the Father, but
> by me. (Jn 14:6 KJV)

In Whom You Abide

Is it wrong? Is it right?
How do I decide?
The choice is determined by
In whom you abide

I trusted him with my heart
And she promised and lied
Your heart was broken by
In whom you abide

I have secrets and hurts
And no one to confide
Your confusion reflects
In whom you abide

You will always feel empty
Until you let go of your pride
Come to Jesus and let Him be
In whom you abide

    If ye abide in me, and my words abide in
you, ye shall ask what ye will, and it shall be done
unto you. (Jn 15:7)

Like Me

If only they could look like me
It would be easy to accept them
Pray my prayers, sing my songs
That would make a sure connection

If only they would dress like me
I'd embrace them with such ease
Accept my insights and ideas
I am not that hard to please

I've had a lot of experience
I am comfortable with self
It is really in their interest
To look to no one else

So God when I convert them
In my image they should be
And if they seem unlike You
Well, at least they look like me

> Woe unto you, scribes and Pharisees, hyp-
> ocrites! for ye compass sea and land to make one
> proselyte, and when he is made, ye make him
> twofold more the child of hell than yourselves.
> (Mt 23:15)

Your Substance

I knew your substance
I knew your frame
Before egg met sperm
I called your name

I made each cell
Divide and grow
Not even your mother
Felt what I did know

As each organ formed
As each limb gained length
As each muscle gained
In bulk and strength

You went from ooze
To person at birth
Before others saw you
I knew your worth

Now you have come forth
You must realize
It is I Who decide
Who lives and dies

So don't forget
And don't forsake
To give thanks and praise
With each breath you take

My substance was not hid from thee, when I was made in secret, and curiously wrought in the lowest parts of the earth. Thine eyes did see my substance, yet being unperfect; and in thy book all my members were written, which in continuance were fashioned, when as yet there was none of them. (Ps 139:15–16)

Into the Hole

I leaped into a deep, deep hole
The risk seemed worth the taking
There was a flashing shiny thing
It was worthless; I was mistaken

The walls were too slick to climb
They were made of cold dark clay
Once inside I realized
I'd never see the light of day

But some nice strangers passing by
Felt pity and asked my name
We don't have gifts to throw down now
But we will send help just the same

A man in priestly apparel
Heard my voice from way down there
Leaned over the dark pit and quickly
Offered his most fervent prayer

Is there no way out? I wondered
Must I live in this hole, this well
I know it is my own fault
Who can deliver me from this hell?

Just as I asked the question
The words still on my tongue
I felt a holy presence say
Dear child, I am the One

No matter how deep the hole
No matter what the cause
When everyone else forsakes you
I hear each time you call

I am the Comforter and Keeper
I know this dark hole's chill
I am light and resurrection
I am life and peace—be still

When it seems there is no way out
When darkness only pervades
Cries of guilt, tears of anguish
Let the I Am invade

He knows that I am tempted
He knows that I do sin
He tells me that the way out
Is first to let Him in

The consequences I do bear
From the wrong that I decide
Jesus steps into the hole
And with me He does abide

> Whither shall I go from thy spirit? or
> whither shall I flee from thy presence?
> If I ascend up into heaven, thou art there:
> if I make my bed in hell, behold, thou art there.
> If I take the wings of the morning, and
> dwell in the uttermost parts of the sea;
> Even there shall thy hand lead me, and thy
> right hand shall hold me.
> If I say, Surely the darkness shall cover me;
> even the night shall be light about me.
> Yea, the darkness hideth not from thee; but
> the night shineth as the day: the darkness and the
> light are both alike to thee. (Ps 139:7–12)

My Enemy Is God

My enemy won't relent
He never lets me win
He keeps reminding me
Of my internal desire to sin

Whenever I choose wrong
He presents me with what's right
He never tires or gives up
He wants to win this fight

I seek to do what is evil
He wants me to do good
His overwhelming power
Cannot be for long withstood

Oh, I know it sounds unreasonable
Indeed more than just odd
My enemy is not the devil
My enemy is God

I have a natural bend to Satan
And inclined naturally to sin
But my Father keeps pursuing me
And refuses to give in

Lest you think the issues are settled
Lest you think over sin you've won
Next time your enemy tempts you
See what words come on your tongue

Can you speak well of those who hate you?
Seek their good and not their harm?
Then you have become God's friend
Close to His heart, under His arm

And the scripture was fulfilled which saith, Abraham believed God, and it was imputed unto him for righteousness: and he was called the Friend of God. (Jas 2:23)

For if, while we were God's enemies, we were reconciled to him through the death of his Son, how much more, having been reconciled, shall we be saved through his life! (Rom 5:10)

Be ye therefore perfect, even as your Father which is in heaven is perfect. (Mt 5:48)

Hide Here

His voice was soft and tender
A sweet whisper in my ear
Whenever you are troubled, child
Come with Me and hide here

If I should die today
No one would shed a tear
How do I love myself?
Come with Me and hide here

I know your disappointment
I am always very near
Don't give up or run away
Come with Me and hide here

> Thou art my hiding place and my shield: I
> hope in thy word. (Ps 119:114 KJV)

Wealthless Are Worthless

Are the wealthless worthless?
Does God know their names?
Do the dispossessed matter?
Or only those rich with fame?

Do the penniless count?
Should the naked stay bare?
Does God even notice?
Does God even care?

When the hungry do faint
When the wounded do cry
Does God intervene
Or stand idly by?

I accuse You, Creator
You should intervene
You watch disasters unfold
You were first on the scene

Then I heard His soft voice
Yes, it matters to Me
Now I give you a choice
You can answer their plea

You can comfort the lost
Provide shelter from cold
You can visit the prisons
Use the advantage you hold

Give the thirsty clean water
Those blind to hope, help them see
Tell the wealthless they are worthy
They are made worthy by Me

> Then shall he answer them, saying, Verily I
> say unto you, Inasmuch as ye did it not to one of
> the least of these, ye did it not to me. (Mt 25:45)

More Mercy and Grace

I look upon the folks I like
And others for whom I have distaste
I choose to admire the former group
Others are wasted mercy and grace

I squandered my health
My wealth I did waste
I asked God's forgiveness
God gave more mercy and grace

I offended and abused
Behind backs and straight to face
Now alone, who will love me?
God gave more mercy and grace

When the world has abandoned
When you have no hiding place
I Am never forsakes you
God gives more mercy and grace

> If I make my bed in hell, behold, thou art
> there. (Ps 139:8 KJV)

You Did Stink

No, I didn't think
And, yes, I ignored
You had such a stink
Who could know You as Lord?

Filthy beyond recognition
Shopping carts, garbage bags
Might I make a suggestion?
Don't dress in those rags

If You want to be praised
Worshipped and adored
Don't look bewildered and crazed
Who wants that kind of Lord?

So clean up Your act
Change motif and attire
Then see me react
I'll even join the church choir

> There was nothing attractive about him, nothing to cause us to take a second look.
> He was looked down on and passed over, a man who suffered, who knew pain firsthand.
> One look at him and people turned away. We looked down on him, thought he was scum.
> (Isaiah 53:2–3)

Thrill or Habit

A little thrill
Not a habit
It could kill
Gotta have it

Just a taste
Where's the harm?
He's passed out
Should alarm

A tiny bit
A little snort
Take the chance
Life is short

Feels so good
Escape what's real
Gotta have it
It did kill

The CDC 2017 cites over seventy thousand drug-related deaths.

> The thief cometh not, but for to steal, and
> to kill, and to destroy: I am come that they might
> have life, and that they might have it more abun-
> dantly. I am the good shepherd: the good shep-
> herd giveth his life for the sheep. (Jn 10:10–11)

Do My Best
2 Timothy 2:15
Colossians 3:23

I am led by my bias
I'm blind to my prejudice
I do God a disservice
When I don't do my best

When I have more to offer
But I offer you less
I deny the power of Christ
When I don't do my best

"Whatever you do, work at it with all your
heart, as working for the Lord, not for human
masters," (Colossians 3:23)

He Remembers, Not Reminds

My Father is wonderful
My Father is kind
My sin He remembers
But He does not remind

He sees every deed
All that crosses my mind
Evil intent He remembers
But He does not remind

When lost deep in sin
No way out to find
He remembers how I got there
But He does not remind

> He will turn again, he will have compassion
> upon us; he will subdue our iniquities; and thou
> wilt cast all their sins into the depths of the sea.
> (Mi 7:19 KJV)

Who I Am

Know Who I am
Know what I do
It is what I, your Lord,
Require of you

I alone Am God
I alone Am true
It's Who I am
It's what I do

Your frets and fears
Cloud Me from view
I am hope and joy
It's what I do

I won't share glory
Won't be number two
I enable perfection
It's what I do

I bring to nothing
Things men pursue
I am the sovereign Creator
It's what I do

Forgiveness and love
Unmerited, not due
It's Who I am
It's what I do

> But God commendeth his love toward us,
> in that, while we were yet sinners, Christ died for
> us. (Rom 5:8 KJV)

I Pretend to Care

When no one is watching
When no one is there
I ignore the poor
I pretend to care

I buy what I want
More than my share
But when they can see
I pretend to care

My pockets are full
Beyond cameras glare
I fill bags and packets
I pretend to care

I live at the fullest
Does it matter what is fair?
Ignore hurting people
I pretend to care

May God forgive
May God forbear
May God have mercy
When I pretend to care

Take heed that ye do not your alms before
men, to be seen of them: otherwise ye have no
reward of your Father which is in heaven.

Therefore when thou doest thine alms, do
not sound a trumpet before thee, as the hypocrites do in the synagogues and in the streets, that

they may have glory of men. Verily I say unto you, They have their reward.

But when thou doest alms, let not thy left hand know what thy right hand doeth:

That thine alms may be in secret: and thy Father which seeth in secret himself shall reward thee openly. (Mt 6:1–4)

Only Bread

I was so very hungry
I just wanted to be fed
I looked at all the tables
And noticed one small setting
Had only simple bread

The others were quite splendid
All luxuriously spread
Every meat and sweet delight
Food to fill the stomach
Drinks to swill the head

I sat down at the feast
Where my appetites had led
Why should I settle for
A table that had nothing
But simple bread?

I ate and ate and ate
Never felt full, but instead
My hunger only increased
Feeling nauseous yet still hungry
Ignoring that simple bread

And so the world allures me
Just as the Lord has said
He who dines with Me
Will never hunger
Taste of My simple bread

I am life and I am light
It was for you that I have bled
I alone can fill your hunger
Eat of Me and live
Taste of My simple bread

> Then Jesus declared, "I am the bread of life. Whoever comes to me will never go hungry, and whoever believes in me will never be thirsty." (Jn 6:35)
>
> Come, all of you who thirst, come to the waters; and you without money, come, buy, and eat! Come, buy wine and milk, without money and without cost! Why spend money on that which is not bread, and your labor on that which does not satisfy? Listen carefully to Me, and eat what is good, and your soul will delight in the richest of foods. (Is 55:1–2)

Lying Down with Fleas

Oh, you mustn't lie down with the fleas
It is sure you will soon be scratching
No matter how clean you might be
These parasites you can't avoid catching

At all costs avoid sleeping in gutters
No matter how convenient it seems
You will smell and look like those others
They are not really on the same team

Character means more than just winning
True victory recognizes the cost
You hold the high ground, and you're grinning
But it's your integrity that you have lost

Can't hold your head high and proclaim
That to get to the top you did wrong
If you betray Christ Jesus's name
Your supposed victory won't be for long

The winds blow strongest at the peak
So before you make the steep climb
Remember your fall will be swift
A dangerous and precipitous decline

> Wherefore let him that thinketh he standeth take heed lest he fall. (1 Cor 10:12)
> Be not deceived: evil communications corrupt good manners. (1 Cor 15:33)

Lead with a Limp

They demean and debase
Call me freak and a gimp
The Father reassured me
You must lead with a limp

But, Lord, I have failed
At most things I attempt
They laugh and ridicule
You must lead with a limp

They take my silence as weakness
Call me slow stupid wimp
It's embarrassing and painful
You must lead with a limp

Jacob's dislocated hip
Paul's thorn, Satan's imp
Moses's stammering tongue
You must lead with a limp

To lead in your strength
Is to let evil tempt
Depend only on Me
You must lead with a limp

> Trust in the Lord with all your heart and
> lean not on your own understanding. (Prv 3:5)
> But God hath chosen the foolish things of
> the world to confound the wise; and God hath
> chosen the weak things of the world to confound
> the things which are mighty. (1 Cor 1:27)

And he said unto me, My grace is sufficient for thee: for my strength is made perfect in weakness. Most gladly therefore will I rather glory in my infirmities, that the power of Christ may rest upon me. (2 Cor 12:9 KJV)

No Measure, Mention, or Merit

God granted me His love
It came without any measure
Overflowing from above
A never-ending treasure

He granted me His mercy
Of my failings made no mention
My faults and selfishness
He refused to give attention

He granted me His grace
Special favor, without merit
Then He gave me this command
Go to the world and share it

My child, the gifts I give
Cost Me a heavy price
Treat them as great value
They cost My Son His life

Don't squander them on self
Don't pretend that you deserve them
Go to the hurting world
Go, my child, and serve them

> For you were called to freedom, brothers.
> Only do not use your freedom as an opportu-
> nity for the flesh, but through love serve one
> another. For the whole law is fulfilled in one
> word: You shall love your neighbor as yourself.
> (Gal 5:13–14)

When Nobody Heard

When nobody heard
The words I did say
When I refused His requests
When I just walked away

When I did have a chance
To say yes but said no
When I refused to assist
Just where did He go?

There was no other resource
No alternative means
When I kept my fists clenched
Did it diminish His dreams?

When I ignored His petitions
Turned my head, closed my eyes
Could I have ever imagined
It was Christ in disguise

> Then shall they also answer him, saying,
> Lord, when saw we thee an hungred, or athirst,
> or a stranger, or naked, or sick, or in prison, and
> did not minister unto thee?
> Then shall he answer them, saying, Verily
> I say unto you, Inasmuch as ye did it not to one
> of the least of these, ye did it not to me. (Mt
> 25:44–45)

Take One

I take one to help me sleep
And another to keep me awake
If I don't good account keep
I am not sure which I should take

It depends on my mood situation
Whom I'm with, what did I drink
If I am to avoid complication
I must take care what I think

For every tablet, capsule, and pill
Different potency, half-life, and strength
Each can extend life or kill
Add joy or make depression intense

So I ask you, dear doctor, clinician
Please listen; please take your time
I am in a dependent position
With your decision my life's on the line

Whom to Hate

The soldier asked his Commander
A question we all could relate
Friend and foe look so much alike
How can we know whom to hate?

There is a slight distinction
In their speech I do detect flaws
If I hold them in prolonged isolation
I'm within confines of present laws

If they shout and make great demands
I can pretend that I just don't hear
After all that's what Jesus would do
He would make them cower in fear

Though some may be good people
The bad ones are hard to detect
But if I let any of them live near me
Who will my interests protect?

The Commander gave a soft retort
You must have read the wrong orders
I am the King of all lands
I don't respect nations or borders

My command is to love My creations
That My love they know and can't doubt
Love them all with genuine compassion
I am *the only One* Who sorts out

If ye oppress not the stranger, the fatherless, and the widow, and shed not innocent blood in this place, neither walk after other gods to your hurt. (Jer 7:6 KJV)

That ye may be the children of your Father which is in heaven: for he maketh his sun to rise on the evil and on the good, and sendeth rain on the just and on the unjust.

For if ye love them which love you, what reward have ye? do not even the publicans the same?

And if ye salute your brethren only, what do ye more than others? do not even the publicans so? Be ye therefore perfect, even as your Father which is in heaven is perfect. (Mt 5:45)

Every Soul Matters

Every soul matters
Each is special to Me
Every life is important
This I want you to see

When he begs on the corner
When her body she bares
He snorts, smokes, or injects
Do more than just stare

Don't demean or disgrace
Don't pretend you don't see
Every life is important
Every soul matters to Me

> Whoso stoppeth his ears at the cry of the
> poor, he also shall cry himself, but shall not be
> heard. (Prv 21:13 KJV)

Now

I worry about the future
The why, when, who, and how
Don't focus on what will come
Pay attention to the now

Self-absorbed, self-centered
At the altar to myself I bow
As if worrying would change the future
Pay attention to the now

Needless concern, sleep lost
Greet the morning with furrowed brow
If God's in control
Pay attention to the now

> Give your entire attention to what God is doing right now, and don't get worked up about what may or may not happen tomorrow. God will help you deal with whatever hard things come up when the time comes. (Mt 6:34 MSG)

Occurred

Has it ever occurred to you
That it never occurred to Me
All the things you decided to do
Are the things I foresaw, I did see

I am neither distraught nor dismayed
Neither confused nor surprised
The events and things you call news
Have long played out in My eyes

You can relax and take a deep breath
Take confidence I am all that is true
I don't predict, set in motion
Nothing is out of My power or purview

> And here's why: God gives out Wisdom free,
> is plainspoken in Knowledge and Understanding.
> He's a rich mine of Common Sense for those who
> live well, a personal bodyguard to the candid and
> sincere. He keeps his eye on all who live honestly,
> and pays special attention to his loyally commit-
> ted ones. (Prv 2:6)

Wasted Mercy and Grace

I know God doesn't see it as such
To Him I show my "poker face"
But to these others I show no pity
Examples of wasted mercy and grace

It is not that I am mean or judgmental
But they seem always out of place
They beg on corners, live in cars
Just more wasted mercy, wasted grace

I sit from a position of comfort
Hunger or want, not even a trace
So how and why should I have pity
For those who flaunt mercy and grace?

> The Lord, the Lord God, merciful and gracious, longsuffering, and abounding in goodness and truth, keeping mercy for thousands, forgiving iniquity and transgression and sin. (Ex 34:6–7)

Both Lion and Lamb

Fueled by greed
It is who I am
Both lust and contentment
Both lion and lamb

My most evil intents
I now understand
My desire controlled by
Both lion and lamb

Resist what is evil
Fulfill God's command
Love those who are weak
Both lion and lamb

Of course preach of hell
And emphasize heaven
Both justice and mercy
Both lion and lamb

> The wolf also shall dwell with the lamb, and
> the leopard shall lie down with the kid; and the
> calf and the young lion and the fatling together;
> and a little child shall lead them. (Is 11:6 KJV)
>
> The thief cometh not, but for to steal, and
> to kill, and to destroy: I am come that they might
> have life, and that they might have it more abun-
> dantly. I am the good shepherd: the good shep-
> herd giveth his life for the sheep. (Jn 10:10–11)

Stop and Start

Stop the anger
Stop the grief
Start the healing
Start relief

Stop the shouting
Stop loud voices
Start the gentle
Start peaceful choices

Stop the me first
Stop my agenda
Start to listen
Start being tender

Stop avoiding
Stop bending the knee
Start with repentance
Start with "God, use me"

> If my people who are called by my name humble themselves, and pray and seek my face and turn from their wicked ways, then I will hear from heaven and will forgive their sin and heal their land. (2 Chr 7:14 ESV)

New Laws

Haven't you noticed the new laws?
Did you take note of the rulings?
Oh yes, there are a few flaws
And yes, it needs some retooling

We are protecting the unborn
We cover those in the womb
Once they come forth, leave them forlorn
Poor nutrition, bad disease, early tomb

Have you noticed our pristine intention?
Our motives are certainly pure
The name of Christ we did mention
As we closed tight the steel prison door

We are doing this all in Your name
We want to make Your love known
If they reject this truth, they're to blame
And this punishment is how it is shown

> This is the kind of fast day I'm after: to break the chains of injustice, get rid of exploitation in the workplace, free the oppressed, cancel debts. What I'm interested in seeing you do is: sharing your food with the hungry, inviting the homeless poor into your homes, putting clothes on the shivering ill-clad, being available to your own families. Do this and the lights will turn on, and your lives will turn around at once. Your righteousness will pave your way. The God of glory will secure your passage. Then when you

pray, God will answer. You'll call out for help and I'll say, "Here I am."

If you get rid of unfair practices, quit blaming victims, quit gossiping about other people's sins, If you are generous with the hungry and start giving yourselves to the down-and-out, Your lives will begin to glow in the darkness, your shadowed lives will be bathed in sunlight. I will always show you where to go. I'll give you a full life in the emptiest of places—firm muscles, strong bones. You'll be like a well-watered garden, a gurgling spring that never runs dry. You'll use the old rubble of past lives to build anew, rebuild the foundations from out of your past. You'll be known as those who can fix anything, restore old ruins, rebuild and renovate, make the community livable again. (Is 58:6–12 MSG)

Black Outrage

Where is the outrage?
Where is the fuss?
It's also a crime
When it's us killing us

Where are the protests?
The riots? The looting?
Why are we silent
When we do the shooting?

Where are the speeches?
The media chatter?
Where are the voices
That cry black lives matter?

Politically correct
Self-righteous, convenient
Moral posturing
I've seen it

If we want to be truthful
This one thing we must
Be enraged and engaged
When it's us killing us

I Will Figure This One Out

I know you are still working
Of this I have no doubt
But since you're moving slow
I will have to figure this one out

The problems are tremendous
In fact, they keep on mounting
At first, just two or three
But now I gave up counting

The riots and the looting
Are a national disaster
The chaos and confusion
Displaced the truth they're after

And the continued contagion
Of a virus no one sees
We are huddled in our homes
Afraid of horrible disease

But God is never silent
You choose not to hear His voice
The continued pain you feel
Is because you made the choice

Of anger and revenge
Hitting back with both your hands
Be still and let Me work
Are the things that I command

> Be still, and know that I am God: I will be
> exalted among the heathen, I will be exalted in
> the earth. (Ps 46:10 KJV)

Sleep Peaceful

I will never sleep peaceful without You
Dreams and visions will dance in my head
The things that I see won't bring joy
They will bring horror and sights that I dread

For only Your soft presence can soothe
As I bury my head on Your breast
All doubts and worries disappear
You alone bring sweet and deep rest

Peaceful sleep not just for the moment
Not just the absence of terror by night
But as I walk through the day without fear
Depending on Your strength and might

Hold me close, dearest Lord, even tighter
Feel Your taste and smell with each breath
Give me peaceful sleep as I live
At life's end, peaceful sleep and not death

> Thou shalt not be afraid for the terror by night; *nor* for the arrow *that* flieth by day. (Ps 91:5 KJV, emphasis added)
> And whoever lives by believing in me will never die. Do you believe this? (Jn 11:26 NIV)
> Peace I leave with you; my peace I give you. I do not give to you as the world gives. Do not let your hearts be troubled and do not be afraid. (Jn 14:27 NIV)

Breathe Again

You ignored your neighbor
You accused your friend
Despite your failure
You can breathe again

You lost your temper
Things you said offend
Despite your failings
You can breathe again

You covet; you're jealous
I count that as sin
Despite your shortcomings
You can breathe again

I have in My power
Your life's beginning and end
It's all up to Me to say
You can breathe again

> *While* I live *will I praise* Jehovah: *I will* sing *praises* unto my God *while* I have any ... *While I have breath I will* give *praise* to the Lord. (Ps 146:2, emphasis added)
>
> Come now, you who say, "Today or tomorrow we will go to this or that city, spend a year there, carry on business, and make a profit." You do not even know what will happen tomorrow! What is your life? You are a mist that appears for a little while and then vanishes. Instead, you ought to say, "If the Lord is willing, we will live and do this or that." (Jas 4:13–15)

A This for My That

I bought a this
To go with my that
Nothing I needed
I have this down pat

I don't buy as I need
I buy what I want
You may call it greed
A tease or a taunt

But if I only purchased
Things I need or consume
Money'd have no purpose
Or so I've assumed

So I bought one of these
Then I bought one of those
Could I do without?
I guess—I suppose

My closet is full
Of this, that, these, those
I could outfit a village
With just half of my clothes

So I purchase my this
To go with my that
Each new suit must
Of course have a new hat

Hurt or Harm

This is meant to alert, not alarm, you
I pray you will know my intent
I'd rather be hurt than to harm you
My harsh words are not what I meant

When I do such an unkind action
When I speak a word that offends
It is too late to make a retraction
The fire once started won't end

Forgive my presumptuous behavior
My actions that caused you such grief
I know it happens too often
This explanation gives no relief

But it does hurt me when I wound you
It is an offense to the God Whom I claim
I will ask my Father in heaven
Help me to love as He loves in His name

Love does no wrong to a neighbor; therefore
love is the fulfilling of the law. (Rom 13:10)

Cleaning Fish

He stood alert and ready
At the water's edge he leaned
He held his knife real steady
Waiting for fish to clean

Once I see them I can clean them
He excitedly proclaimed
Now don't bother me; I'm busy
He turned around, took aim

I was puzzled and dumbfounded
I couldn't begin to understand
How a man could try to clean fish
When he had none in his hand

I couldn't let him stay there
Living under the false notion
Explained you must first catch them
Whether river, lake, or ocean

I am a disciple of the Master
Go fishing, He commanded
Let the Holy Spirit cleanse
That is how the Lord has planned it

> And he saith unto them, Follow me, and I
> will make you fishers of men. (Mt 4:19 KJV)

My Bride

My bride has many lovers
Gives in easily to distraction
I died so she discovers
I must be her one attraction

She seeks and hungers for affection
Not just meeting daily needs
The world gives misdirection
And fleshly appetites feed

I have called her to repentance
To redeem and sanctify
I expected her resistance
And so I had to die

My bride will reflect My essence
And My Father will take delight
When I bring her to His presence
She brings people to His light

> And I John saw the holy city, new Jerusalem,
> coming down from God out of heaven, prepared
> as a bride adorned for her husband. (Rv 21:2
> KJV)

The Helm

Joshua 1:9
Isaiah 45:7

The world is in constant chaos
Mankind is indeed overwhelmed
I'm troubled by who holds the rudder
I focus on who is at the helm

Crime and corruption are unceasing
Evil men reign in this realm
Steering the world to greater conflict
Remember who is at the helm

My personal life seems out of control
Heartbreak and disappointment overwhelm
I don't give up but let go of the rudder
I surrender to the Master at the helm

> The men were amazed and asked, "What
> kind of man is this? Even the winds and the
> waves obey him!" (Matthew 8:27)

Sweet Sleep

The sweetest sleep
When I rest my head
A clear good conscience
That's the finest bed

When the day is over
Well worked and fed
No regrets, no worries
That's the finest bed

Sweet sleep comes
When the Lord has said
Well done, my child
That's the finest bed

I laid me down and slept; I awaked; for the Lord sustained me. (Ps 3:5 KJV)

Therefore when thou doest thine alms, do not sound a trumpet before thee, as the hypocrites do in the synagogues and in the streets, that they may have glory of men. Verily I say unto you, They have their reward.

But when thou doest alms, let not thy left hand know what thy right hand doeth:

That thine alms may be in secret: and thy Father which seeth in secret himself shall reward thee openly. (Mt 6:2–4)

I Have Complaints

I read the bad news
What's true and what ain't
Wars, starvation, and strife
All I have are complaints

My carpet, wrong color
Doesn't match the wall paint
People living in shelters
I have complaints

My suit out of style
My tie has a small taint
People are naked and hungry
I have complaints

I pretend sensitivity
I am a wannabe saint
I tell God to please listen
I have complaints

And Moses said, "When the Lord gives you in the evening meat to eat and in the morning bread to the full, because the Lord has heard your grumbling that you grumble against him—what are we? Your grumbling is not against us but against the Lord." (Ex 16:8)

Others

What should I do with these riches?
The abundance under firm lock and key
I want you to help those who have nothing
I want you to set others free

What should I do with my health?
Each limb, each sense, full faculty
I want you to strengthen the lame
I want you to set others free

What should I do with my time?
With each tick of the clock life does flee
I want you to spend moments with the lonely
I want you to set others free

For nothing you have is yours
Every breath you hold is from Me
I give them to you to help someone
I want you to set others free

Just as I declared in the temple
I send you to the world to show Me
Heal the sick; visit the lonely, the captive
I want you to set others free

> The Spirit of the Lord is upon me, because
> he hath anointed me to preach the gospel to the
> poor; he hath sent me to heal the brokenhearted,
> to preach deliverance to the captives, and recov-
> ering of sight to the blind, to set at liberty them
> that are bruised, To preach the acceptable year of
> the Lord. (Lk 4:18–19)

After

After the naked are clothed
After the hungry have meat
After you comfort the lonely
I want you to wash dirty feet

After the wounded have healed
After they no longer weep
Look for the weary, downtrodden
I want you to help them get sleep

After the confused get an answer
After the lost find a way
After those in darkness find light
Listen closely to what I now say

Your chores and duty don't end
Just because you accomplished these tasks
You are My servant; I bought you
Mine are commands; I don't ask

Because after this life is over
After you have drawn your last breath
My servants don't seek rewards here
They come home with Me and do rest

> Will any one of you who has a servant
> plowing or keeping sheep say to him when he
> has come in from the field, "Come at once and
> recline at table"? Will he not rather say to him,
> "Prepare supper for me, and dress properly, and
> serve me while I eat and drink, and afterward you
> will eat and drink"?

Does he thank the servant because he did what was commanded? So you also, when you have done all that you were commanded, say, "We are unworthy servants; we have only done what was our duty." (Lk 17:7–10)

Grown-Up Jesus

My agenda is in danger
My cover is now blown
The Baby in the manger
Is now all fully grown

He was easy to admire
To cuddle and to hold
But now I've no desire
This grown-up man to hold

He asks a lot of questions
Like all little children do
He ignores my clear suggestions
As if He knows the answers too

As a baby I adored Him
At the end of the last year
But now I just ignore Him
So one thing seems real clear

He is fully grown and complete
He now commands and expects
That anyone who competes
He says He will reject

The Babe once in a manger
Is now all fully grown
To keep me from sin's danger
He wants my life to own

Surrender to this King
Bow to Him not for a season
He alone salvation brings
Submission is the way to please Him

> Come unto me, all ye that labour and are heavy laden, and I will give you rest.
> Take my yoke upon you, and learn of me; for I am meek and lowly in heart: and ye shall find rest unto your souls. (Mt 11:28–29)

Leftovers to Jesus

I gave my leftovers to Jesus
I said to myself, "Jesus won't mind
After all if He is really hungry
He will see my actions as kind"

Clothing that I am not wearing
Shoes with a scuff here and there
After all I am indeed sharing
Without me His feet would be bare

I had a few coins in my pocket
Stuff I don't consider as cash
When traffic slows down at a stop sign
I'll give Jesus a few if He asks

A lot of good stuff I'm not using
And this I know to be true
It is no real value to me
I can always buy something new

> "When you say, 'The altar of God is not important anymore; worship of God is no longer a priority,' that's defiling. And when you offer worthless animals for sacrifices in worship, animals that you're trying to get rid of—blind and sick and crippled animals—isn't that defiling? Try a trick like that with your banker or your senator—how far do you think it will get you?" God-of-the-Angel-Armies asks you. (Mal 1:7–8)

How Far

It is not how high you've risen
it is not how much you've gained
Our God makes His decision
Based on whether you let Him reign

It is not how far you fell
How deep you were in sin
Our God keeps you from hell
Based on whether you let Him in

Many good with great resource
Reputations and fine deeds
Will find within this discourse
Only Christ can fill their needs

Those impoverished and lonely
Who despair, spirits hurting
Will find comfort in Christ only
From eternity this is certain

Don't measure your salvation
Based on personal observation
How far you fall and how high you rise
Only God has this information

Look beyond your situation
Ignore your status, high or low
God sees your reputation
And He determines where you go

For John the Baptist came to you showing you the right path to take, and you would not believe him; but the tax collectors and the prostitutes believed him. Even when you saw this, you did not later change your minds and believe him. (Mt 21:32)

Somebody Has to Die

He seemed ever so serious
He looked me squarely in the eye
In order for them to believe us
Then somebody has to die

We have a lot to keep hidden
We need a very good alibi
If this secret is just between us
Then somebody has to die

The truth must never be known
And so just between you and I
In order for me to survive
Then somebody has to die

I have learned over the years
When someone wants me to lie
They will abandon me when convenient
After all, somebody has to die

> An honest witness does not deceive but a
> false witness pours out lies. (Prv 14:5)

End with Love

When the arguments won't stop
With no end of push and shove
If we want real resolution
We have to end with love

We refuse to leave our corners
Best take off the boxing gloves
Meet at the center of the ring
We have to end with love

We can win all the debates
So we will be well spoken of
But if we want to win the heart
We have to end with love

Love never keeps a score
Leaves that to God above
Forbear, forgive, embrace
We have to end with love

> Love is patient and kind; love does not envy
> or boast; it is not arrogant or rude. It does not
> insist on its own way; it is not irritable or resent-
> ful it does not rejoice at wrongdoing, but rejoices
> with the truth. Love bears all things, believes all
> things, hopes all things, endures all things. (1
> Cor 13:4–7)

No Worth in You

He spoke with great conviction
Never stopped, never stuttered
Not a drop of sweat or perspiration
As if God Himself had uttered

I see no worth in you
Your kind are not like us
You worship other gods
I can't believe or trust

The way you dress and speak
Your festivals and songs
Make me feel uncomfortable
Must be evil and quite wrong

Go back from where you came
I won't share this truth I know
That Jesus Christ is Savior
No mercy to you I show

I deserve His love and mercy
I am entitled to endless grace
You were born eternally dammed
A heathen people, a cursed race

As I listened, I was shaken
I felt disappointed and defeated
Could I really be mistaken?
Does Christ agree with what is tweeted?

Are some entitled to forgiveness?
Does it matter what they say?
If they hate me, is it wrong?
Does it matter if I pray?

Never and Always
John 6:37

Never turned out
Never betrayed
Never left feeling
Alone or dismayed

Never belittled
Never offended
Never ignored
Always befriended

Never kept worried
Never made shamed
Never felt burdened
Unwanted, unclaimed

Always feel welcomed
Always embraced
Always at home
In His love and His grace

> Come unto me, all ye that labour and are
> heavy laden, and I will give you rest.(Matthew
> 11:28)

Feed the Roots

Every day above the ground
Affirms the simple truth
God granted you see the flowers
Tomorrow, you feed the roots

Each breath, every heartbeat
Is grace, and here's the proof
Today you eat the harvest
Tomorrow, you feed the roots

All of life is a circle
Every seedling has a shoot
One day you and I
Will have a chance to feed the roots

> For all flesh is as grass, and all the glory of
> man as the flower of grass. The grass withereth,
> and the flower thereof falleth away:
> But the word of the Lord endureth for
> ever. And this is the word which by the gospel is
> preached unto you. (1 Pt 1:24–25 KJV)

Sweat
Joshya 1:9

With sweat your body's drenched
Trying to solve this on your own
While you worry who's on the bench
I'm still seated on the throne

You have your personal choices
Your political views are known
I'm the Judge Who hears all voices
I'm still seated on the throne

Don't ask a chair or stool or pew
Or soft couch filled with foam
To comfort or protect you
I'm still seated on the throne

Human justice is for a season
Always confuses right and wrong
When there is no rhyme or reason
I'm still seated on the throne

Despair and human heartbreak
Ezekiel saw fields of bones
I will never leave nor forsake
I'm still seated on the throne

> I am Alpha and Omega, the beginning
> and the ending, saith the Lord, which is, and
> which was, and which is to come, the Almighty.
> (Revelation 1:8)

Having Less

If there's one thing I've learned in this life
If there is one thing that I must confess
In all my efforts to have more
I end up having much less

I end scheming, gaining and getting
Collecting there is so much stress
In competing and trying to show who is better
I end up missing out on the best

Of course, I am well fed
I am fabulously dressed
Well adorned with the accessories
But of peace, I have much less

Until I learn obedience
I will never pass this test
I must find my joy in Jesus
God accepts nothing less

Come, all you who are thirsty, come ot the waters; and you without money, come, buy, and eat! Come, buy wine and milk without money and without cost! [2]Why spend money on that which is not bread, and your labor on that which does not satisfy? Listen carefully to Me, and eat what is good, and your soul will delight in the richest of foods.(Isaiah 55:1-2)

What's Eating You

The psychiatrist and dietitian
Have opposing points of view
One asks "What did you eat?"
The other "What's eating you?"

And so this age-old proverb
Has a spin that is quite new
You are not what you eat
But you are what's eating you

Your emotions and feelings
The heated language that you spew
Reflect the fierce passions
Of what is really eating you

You dislike those other people
You despise everything they do
The mere fact they exist
Is what is really eating you

So you ruminate and brood
Your emotions simmer and stew
You can't even enjoy life
Because this is eating you

So take this old proverb
Give it a twist that is new
You are not what you eat
You are what's eating you

Finally, brethren, whatsoever things are true, whatsoever things are honest, whatsoever things are just, whatsoever things are pure, whatsoever things are lovely, whatsoever things are of good report; if there be any virtue, and if there be any praise, think on these things. (Phil 4:8)

God Lowers Standards

Whores, convicts, and queers
Conmen, fraudsters, and fiends
The very people Jesus draws near
The same folk I still demean

Not that Christ accepts the behavior
Nor does He claim them as good
But He still wants to be their Savior
Something I've not understood

How can the Holy Redeemer
The Perfect Lamb, the Divine
Invite these misfits, these sinners
Into the same heaven as mine?

How can He overlook and forgive?
Why allow such evil and sin?
He answered, I lowered the standard
To give you a chance to get in

The Holy Spirit's quiet response
If I only chose those who deserve
You wouldn't be on the list either
Heaven is for sinners reserved

Sinners who surrendered, repented
These are the ones welcome here
They have rejected their earthly lifestyle
No longer whores nor convicts nor queers

Know ye not that the unrighteous shall not inherit the kingdom of God? Be not deceived: neither fornicators, nor idolaters, nor adulterers, nor effeminate, nor abusers of themselves with mankind, Nor thieves, nor covetous, nor drunkards, nor revilers, nor extortioners, shall inherit the kingdom of God.

And such were some of you: but ye are washed, but ye are sanctified, but ye are justified in the name of the Lord Jesus, and by the Spirit of our God. (1 Cor 6:9–11 KJV)

Those Other People

I wonder why the worry
I wonder why the fuss
But then I see those people
Don't even look like us

We have limited social services
Can't begin to meet the need
And after all those people
They really like to breed

We are to guard our resources
Part of the public trust
We must not let those people
Take advantage of us

At every depot, airport, dock
Every train or plane or bus
Offload another hundred
Of those different from us

And so we should be careful
Whom to watch and whom to trust
Because we were once those people
And now we are part of us

> Love ye therefore the stranger: for ye were
> strangers in the land of Egypt. (Dt 10:19 KJV)

Kill All the Evil People

Let's kill all the evil people
Those intent on doing bad
For the evil they have done
Or the evil thoughts they've had

Let's kill them while they sleep
Before they open their eyes
Killing is most efficient
When it happens by surprise

Let's do this hastily
Don't make such a fuss
Let's kill all the evil people
That means…even us

There is none that understandeth, there is
none that seeketh after God. (Rom 3:11 KJV)

Just a Smidgen

Just a taste
I won't take too much
Don't want to waste

Just a quick try
A teeny little bit
Won't be a habit
Can always quit

A tight short skirt
A brief quick glance
Who can it hurt?
It's not romance

Just a smidgen
Won't even swallow
If only I knew
What would follow

Decision made
The deed is done
Now haunted by sin
I've nowhere to run

But every man is tempted, when he is
drawn away of his own lust, and enticed. Then
when lust hath conceived, it bringeth forth sin:
and sin, when it is finished, bringeth forth death.
(Jas 1:14–15 KJV)

For the wages of sin is death; but the gift of
God is eternal life through Jesus Christ our Lord.
(Rom 6:23 KJV)

And when the woman saw that the tree was good for food, and that it was pleasant to the eyes, and a tree to be desired to make one wise, she took of the fruit thereof, and did eat, and gave also unto her husband with her; and he did eat. (Gn 3:6 KJV)

A Dry Cough

First, a dry cough
Then a wet sneeze
And without even knowing
I had spread the disease

A low-grade slight fever
A subtle quick chill
And without realizing
Someone is killed

It's my body, my civil right
My personal choice
For this I will fight
Won't silence my voice

Don't try to persuade
I have personal reasons
If someone dies with me
It is our time and our season

Achoo! and God bless you
I spit out that snot
I refuse the vaccine
I am afraid of the shot

Washing hands, wearing a mask
I will attempt to comply
But injection with needles
Please, don't even try

Feel Safer—He's Dead

I woke up this morning and read
Feel safer now that he's dead
Feel safe in the malls
In school classrooms and halls
That's right—there is nothing to dread

But somehow this doesn't ring true
Not quite sure what I should do
Stay home behind curtains
'Till I can be quite certain
He is not pursuing me; he wants you

Of course there's no cause for alarm
Only certain people mean us real harm
They dress in odd fashion
Have religions with passion
We can strike them before they rearm

The problem with this kind of plan
It puts a never-ending demand
If we are to survive
We must keep hate alive
And destroy him to the last man

There is the alternative way
But for that all men must obey
If we all want to live
We must learn to forgive
We will give account on the last day

> For all that take the sword shall perish by
> the sword. (Mt 26:52)

Lord, Make Me Rich

Lord, make me rich
In the year 2020
Where I have but little
Lord, please give me plenty

The wealth of great mercy
Treasures of unlimited love
Rich with forgiveness
Like Yours from above

Lord, help me set
A most sumptuous table
Giving generously to
Those who are less able

Lord, let me dress
In the most fabulous fashion
Clothe me with garments
Of your grace and compassion

Lord, give me only
Things of great price
I want others to see
The wealth found in Christ

> Charge them that are rich in this world, that they be not highminded, nor trust in uncertain riches, but in the living God, who giveth us richly all things to enjoy That they do good, that they be rich in good works, ready to distribute. (1 Tm 6:17–18)

The Same List, Lord

It's the same list, Lord
Just read it
That way I won't have
To repeat it

I will cut back on sin
Stop cussing again
Only buy stuff
When I need it

It's the same list, Lord
Don't ignore it
New Year's resolution
Don't score it

Yes, I likely will fail
But who's gonna tell
I'll hold on to this list
For next year, I will store it

> When you make a promise to the Lord your God, don't be slow to pay everything you promised. The Lord your God will demand that you pay it. You will sin if you don't pay what you promised. (Dt 23:21)

A Passion for Lepers and Whores

I have a passion for lepers and whores
The people the world does abuse
The people most everyone ignores
Those who are weak and easy to use

I have a passion for those left behind
The disabled, the weak, and the frail
It is they who are first on my mind
And so it is you I compel

Go search for the lonely and lost
Look for those who feel left out
I did pay the ultimate cost
That is what My death was about

I died for the worthless, the fools
Because by My Father's measure
He sees them as precious jewels
They comprise heaven's true treasure

> But God hath chosen the foolish things of the world to confound the wise; and God hath chosen the weak things of the world to confound the things which are mighty. (1 Cor 1:27)
>
> For I was an hungered and ye gave me meat: I was thirsty and ye gave me drink: I was naked and ye clothed me I was sick and ye visited me I was in prison and ye came up to me. (Mt 25:35–36)

Fate, Fear, and Faith

Fate came to my door
Said, "I have bad news today
Why don't you let me in
And hear what I have to say?"

I stopped and stayed real quiet
I tried hard to ignore
I scrunched down behind the couch
Lying silent on the floor

But fate just kept on knocking
"I know that you are here"
I knew someone had to answer
So I beckoned my friend fear

But just as fear arose
To go and welcome fate
Faith said, "No, I'll do this"
And he did not hesitate

Faith met fate at the door
And made him turn around
Saying in no uncertain terms
"Fate, you are out of bounds"

With those words fate scattered
Looking for another home
And he took fear with him
So he would not be alone

I then sat back relaxed
In a peaceful atmosphere
When those two come a knocking
I tell them only faith lives here

> For I am persuaded, that neither death, nor
> life, nor angels, nor principalities, nor powers, nor
> things present, nor things to come, Nor height,
> nor depth, nor any other creature, shall be able
> to separate us from the love of God, which is in
> Christ Jesus our Lord. (Rom 8:38–39 KJV)

Another Pharaoh

Lord, send us another Pharaoh
Who supports things that we believe
Who backs the causes we like
We can't wait for this one to leave

A Pharaoh who will easily comply
A leader in whom we can trust
And not like this present guy
He should look and think like us

God answered this selfish request
You speak with arrogant pride
Until your sin is addressed
Your evil is like the other side

I send every Pharaoh disdained
The choices are Mine, not yours
And I will do it again and again
I do right—I don't even scores

> Now there arose up a new king over Egypt, which knew not Joseph. (Ex 1:8 KJV)
> And he changeth the times and the seasons: he removeth kings, and setteth up kings: he giveth wisdom unto the wise, and knowledge to them that know understanding. (Dn 2:21 KJV)
> Jesus answered, Thou couldest have no power at all against me, except it were given thee from above: therefore he that delivered me unto thee hath the greater sin. (Jn 19:11 KJV)

Your Own Dirt

I told the preacher man
I tried so not to hurt him
Would a good God create man
And then suddenly desert him?

Just let me in the lab
I can show you I can do it
As for this creation
There's really nothing to it

Creation is a myth
A story of no worth
The worlds just came to be
Evolution gave us birth

The preacher unimpressed
Said, Don't you be so curt
If you plan to do creation
You start with your own dirt

> Then the Lord answered Job out of the whirlwind, and said, Who is this that darkeneth counsel by words without knowledge? Gird up now thy loins like a man; for I will demand of thee, and answer thou me. Where wast thou when I laid the foundations of the earth? declare, if thou hast understanding. (Jb 38:1–4 KJV)

Vilify the Vulnerable

They cluster at the border
They stink, and they are dirty
They disrupt the civil order
Unlike us, they are unworthy

Illiterate and unclean
Unskilled and dirt poor
We are perfectly pristine
Yet these folks are at our door

They want the things we have
The things we value most
Abundance and prosperity
Possessions which we boast

In order to preserve
And in order to secure
The lifestyles we deserve
To keep our culture pure

We must stop this bad invasion
We must keep these people out
Use the tactics Jesus used
"Secure the borders," He would shout

> Be sure to welcome strangers into your home.
> By doing this, some people have welcomed angels
> as guests, without even knowing it. (Heb 13:2)
> The foreigner who resides with you must be
> like a native citizen among you; so you must love
> him as yourself, because you were foreigners in the
> land of Egypt. I am the Lord your God. (Lv 19:34)

About the Author

Dr. Michael Johnson and his wife Dr. Kay Johnson have been involved in overseas missionary work since 1984. They were accepted to full-time work with World Gospel Mission in 1989. Their ministry has taken them to several sites in Africa, including the Sudan, the Democratic Republic of the Congo (formerly Zaire), Ethiopia, Uganda, Kenya (where they worked for twenty years), and Haiti (short-term work).

Their work in Kenya included working in mission hospitals (Tenwek, Kijabe, and St. Mary's), where Michael functioned as surgeon and Kay's responsibilities included administration and finance. God gave them the ministries of The Least of These and A Prepared Place, allowing them to work with a variety of indigenous Kenyan organizations. That work included providing food, clothing, and education, and in-country adoption services for orphans. They were able to help build self-sustainable sources of food and water for rural populations. Their supporters helped fund the building of a full primary school and pay for secondary and college education for orphans. The Johnsons returned to the United States in 2010 and currently reside in Delaware. Their ministries now include healthcare for the "medically indigent" in Philadelphia at the Miriam Medical Clinics, which they cofounded; counseling to the incarcerated; and, as the medical director for the Hope Pregnancy Center in Philadelphia, providing the resources to help women and girls make life-affirming decisions.

Michael received his undergraduate degree at Lawrence University in Wisconsin. He then attended medical school at the University of Michigan, in Ann Arbor, Michigan. And Kay is a graduate of the Walden University MBA program in Minneapolis, Minnesota. Both Kay and Michael were awarded Doctorates in Humane Letters from Eastern University in St. Davids Pennsylvania. During their forty-four of marriage, God has blessed them with four (now adult) children and seven grandchildren. Their home church is the Tasker Street Missionary Baptist Church in Philadelphia.

This book is one of several publications including articles and books pursuing the infinite intimacy of knowing our Creator God through the new birth found only in Jesus the Christ. Dr. Johnson's most widely read book **Making the Blind Man Lame** explores the challenges of racial and cultural issues in Christian missions. That book is based upon the Johnsons' 20-year experiences while serving in Kenya. Support for their work can be made https://miriammedical.org/

More of Dr. Johnson's writing can be found at the blog site thosepeculiarjohnsons.org.

Printed in the USA
CPSIA information can be obtained
at www.ICGtesting.com
CBHW032109140324
5259CB00001B/4

9 781685 704568